Fantastic!

Student's Book 4

Jane Revell • Carol Skinner

Macmillan

Contents

Review	Vocabulary	Grammar	Features
 **Unit 1** Pages 4–11	look at pictures, play the guitar, cook, drink sodas engineer, dancer, athlete, vet bear, lizard, owl, fox insect, reptile, bird, animal	Present progressive: all forms Past simple: was / were Future: going to all forms Some / Any + countable and uncountable nouns	**Song** In the Supermarket! **Cross-curricular** Science **Value:** Learn why animals are important to us.
 **Unit 2** Pages 12–19	dress, school uniform, sweatsuit, tennis shoes go shopping, make the food, clean up, decorate the room carnival costume, cowboy hat, Halloween costume, pajamas hot, cold, wet, dry	She always plays games. Sam often sings. Does Joe always have his pets at parties? Yes, he does. No, he doesn't. He never goes shopping.	**Song** It's My Birthday **Cross-curricular** Science **Value:** Celebrating is fun!
 Reading Time Pages 20–21	The "Yes" Game		
 **Unit 3** Pages 22–29	pick, drop, collect, try start, stop, fry, play wild animals, farm and ranch animals, pets sail, arrive, people, land	She picked apples. He tried to brush the horses. She dropped some eggs. Sara didn't work. Did you work all day? No, we didn't. What did you do? I fried some eggs.	**Song** In the Countryside **Cross-curricular** History **Value:** Enjoy outdoor activities!
 **Unit 4** Pages 30–37	made, bought, went, did weekend, soccer, softball, sports stadium draw, write, read, clean cave, stone, skin, jewelry	Last Monday, I went to the movie theater. Did you go to the movies last week? Yes, we did. What did Joe do last Sunday? He brushed his dog.	**Song** Aliens **Cross-curricular** History **Value:** Learn about your history.
Reading Time Pages 38–39	The Lion's Friend		
 **Unit 5** Pages 40–47	fast, slow, pretty, young colorful, expensive, beautiful, comfortable feet, head, body, arms cheetah, chimpanzee, panda, giraffe	Millie is faster than Minnie. Is Sid older than her? The new coat is more expensive than the old coat.	**Song** What's for Dinner? **Cross-curricular** Geography **Value:** Help to save wild animals.

	Vocabulary	Grammar	Features
 Unit 6 Pages 48–55	Japan, Spain, India, Russia good, bad, excellent, terrible Brazil, the United States, Germany, Australia skiing, hockey, water-skiing, rugby	I love wearing this costume. Do you like painting? Joe's bad at dancing.	**Song** Friends Around the World **Cross-curricular** Geography **Value:** Respect people around the world.
 Reading Time Pages 56–57	The King of the Animals		
 Unit 7 Pages 58–65	skateboard, baseball bat, rollerblades, skates glasses, eyes, teeth, legs pop star, movie star, soccer player, TV star cousin, aunt, uncle, family	This baseball bat is yours/mine/hers/his. The skates are ours/theirs. Whose book is this? It's Penny's. Whose rollerblades are these? They're Sam's and Sara's.	**Song** Whose Kitten Is It? **Cross-curricular** Social Studies **Value:** Love your family.
 Unit 8 Pages 66–73	idea, playground, strict, mice English, math, history, geography art, science, physical education, music modern, slippers, special, ballet	You must wear your school uniform. You mustn't play soccer. What does she look like? She's better at math. She's the best in the class.	**Song** At School **Cross-curricular** Social Studies **Value:** Follow school rules.
 Reading Time Pages 74–75	The Unhappy Ghost		
 Unit 9 Pages 76–83	dog house, wood, nails, screws gram, kilo, 250 grams, liter, 500 grams a bag, a bottle, a can, a jar grow, lose, bite, chew	There's too much wood. There are too many nails. There aren't enough screws. There isn't enough paint. How much milk is there? How many socks are there?	**Song** At the Dentist **Cross-curricular** Social Studies **Value:** Take care of your teeth.
 Unit 10 Pages 84–91	windsurfing, ice-cream cone, money, home speak English, use a computer, write a story, play softball play chess, ride a horse, catch a fish, make the bed crawl, walk sideways, slide, climb	Why don't we go water-skiing? I could swim last year, but I couldn't dive. Could you ride a bike when you were seven?	**Song** Move Around! **Cross-curricular** Science **Value:** Protect ocean animals.
Reading Time Pages 92–93	The Rich King		
Consolidation Pages 94–95	English Is Fantastic!		

Unit 1

Lesson 1

1 look at pictures (v)   play the guitar (v)   cook (v)   drink sodas (v)

2 Listen and read. Then act it out.

Hi, Bob! What are you doing?

Hi, Sara! Welcome back! We're looking at my pictures from last year.

Look at Sam! He's playing the guitar and Joe's cooking!

And we're drinking sodas!

3 Ask and answer.

What's Sam doing? — He's playing the guitar.

What's Sara doing? — She's drinking a soda.

Unit 1 Lesson 2

1 Listen and read. Then act it out.

What are you doing, Sam?

I'm putting Bob's pictures on the wall. Look at us at the bowling alley. That's me! And that's Bob! You're behind him with your pet snake.

Say! That's me!

2 Complete and answer.

him   them   her   me

1 Look at Joe! Who's standing in front of __him__?   __Bob__

2 Look at Penny! Who's standing behind _____?   _____

3 I'm Emma! Who's sitting next to _____?   _____

4 There's Emma and Penny. Who's between _____?   _____

3 Listen and say.

A big black bowling ball.

Unit 1 — Lesson 3

1 engineer (n)   dancer (n)   athlete (n)   vet (n)

2 Listen and read.

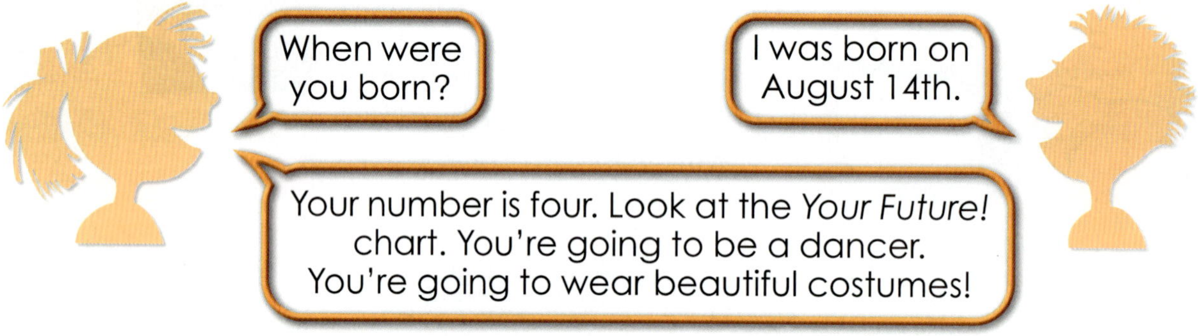

- When were you born?
- I was born on August 14th.
- Your number is four. Look at the *Your Future!* chart. You're going to be a dancer. You're going to wear beautiful costumes!

Write the numbers of the month and day: 8 and 14
Add the numbers 8 + 14:   22
Add the numbers again 2 + 2:   4

Your Future!

1	farmer	have / 70 cows	2	engineer	have / lots of tools
3	chef	have / three aprons	4	dancer	wear / beautiful costumes
5	athlete	go / to competitions	6	singer	sing / lots of music
7	teacher	have / 20 students	8	writer	write / lots of books
9	vet	have / lots of animals	10	artist	paint / 30 pictures

3 Now find your number and say "your future."

- My number is … I'm going to …

Unit 1 Lesson 4 — I Know...

1 Complete and learn.

Language Check

NOW	THE FUTURE
1 <u>She's eating.</u>	2 <u>She's going to</u> eat.
3 _____	4 It's _____ rain.
5 _____	6 He's _____ fly.

2 Look at the pictures. Complete the questions and answer.

1  Is / a cookie / Fifi / eating ?
<u>Is Fifi eating a cookie?</u>   <u>No, she isn't.</u>

2  Is / raining / it ?
_____   _____

3  Is / going to / rain / it ?
_____   _____

Word Fun 3 Write two words in each list.

INSTRUMENTS	EATING	ANIMALS
guitar	knife	snake

Unit 1
Lesson 5

We're going to make a game in school today.
We need **paper** and **markers**!
Hooray, hooray, hooray!

1 bear (n)   lizard (n)   owl (n)   fox (n)

2 Make a game.

Find two pieces of paper. On each, draw some trees in the woods. Write "Yesterday" on one and "Today" on the other.

Draw and color one, two, or three bears, lizards, owls, and foxes in the "Yesterday" picture.

Draw and color one, two, or three bears, lizards, owls, and foxes in the "Today" picture. Put different numbers of the animals than you have in the "Yesterday" picture.

3 Play "Find the difference."

Yesterday there wasn't one owl in the woods. Today there's one owl in the woods.

That's right. Good job!

Unit 1 — Lesson 6

1 Match. Then write the plural or write no plural.

1 banana
2 water
3 apple
4 toothpaste
5 orange
6 honey

bananas
no plural
_____
_____
_____
_____

2 Listen and read. Then sing the song.

In the Supermarket!

Are there any eggs in the house?

Where? Oh, where?

There aren't any eggs in the house.

But, there are some eggs over there …

In the supermarket!

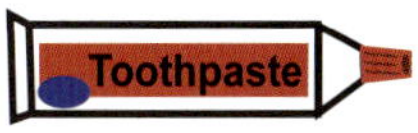

Is there any bread in the house?

Where? Oh, where?

There isn't any bread in the house.

But, there's some bread over there …

In the supermarket!

3 Write your song.

Are there any **pears** …   Is there any **toothpaste** …

Unit 1 · Lesson 7 — Science

1  insect (n)   reptile (n)   bird (n)   animal (n)

2 Read and label.

> penguin ~~caterpillar~~ dinosaur snake butterfly ostrich

caterpillar   _____

Insects, reptiles, and birds are animals. First there were insects, then there were dinosaurs. Insects have six legs and they often have wings. A butterfly is an insect. This beautiful butterfly was a caterpillar first.

_____   _____

Birds have feathers and two legs. An owl is a bird. Some birds can fly, but ostriches and penguins are birds and they can't fly.

_____   _____

Millions of years ago there were lots of reptiles. Dinosaurs were reptiles. The dinosaurs were big and dangerous. Some reptiles today, like some snakes and crocodiles, are big and dangerous too.

3 Write the animals' names in Activity 2 in your notebook.

INSECTS	REPTILES	BIRDS

Values! Learn why animals are important to us.

Unit 1 — Lesson 8

Fantastic Fun!

Stone and Bone
Act it out!

- Who's making that horrible noise?
- Dina!
- What are you doing?
- I'm playing rock music.

Dictation Time!

Listen and circle.

1.  **Yes, there are.** / No, there aren't.
2.  Yes, there are. / No, there aren't.
3.  Yes, there is. / No, there isn't.
4.  Yes, there is. / No, there isn't.
5.  Yes, there is. / No, there isn't.

My Writing

Put in the capital letters, question marks, and periods.

1. are snakes reptiles
   <u>Are snakes reptiles?</u>

2. i was born on january 25th
   _____

3. there isn't any water
   _____

4. is it going to rain
   _____

Write the new words in your **Fantastic Dictionary**.

Unit 2 — Lesson 1

Look and Learn
She **always** plays games.
Sam **often** sings.

1 dress (n)   school uniform (n)   sweatsuit (n)   tennis shoes (n)

2 Listen and read.

Sara always has a party on Saturday evenings! She always wears a beautiful dress. Sam often sings. What a noise! Penny often wears her school uniform to parties! Emma always plays games and wears a sweatsuit and tennis shoes.

3 Correct the sentences in your notebook.

1 Sara often wears a beautiful dress.
   Sara always wears a beautiful dress.

2 Sam always sings at parties.

3 Emma often wears tennis shoes.

4 Penny always wears her school uniform.

Say! What a noise!

Unit 2 Lesson 2

Look and Learn

Does Joe **always** have his pets at parties?
Yes, he **does**.
No, he **doesn't**.

1 Listen and read. Then act it out.

Does Joe always have his pets at parties?

Yes, he does. And his dog always eats a lot!

2 Look at the table. Ask and answer.

Does Joe always eat a lot?

Yes, he does.

	YES	NO
(always) eat a lot	✓	
(often) sing and dance		✓
(often) do tricks		✓
(always) wear jeans	✓	

3 Listen and say.

She always plays in the rain.

Unit 2 — Lesson 3

Look and Learn

He **never** goes shopping.

 **1**   go shopping (v)   make the food (v)
  clean up (v)   decorate the room (v)

2 Ask and answer. Circle your friend's answers.

DO YOU HAVE GOOD PARTIES?

1 Before your party do you …
  go shopping?   A always   B often   C never
  make the food?   A always   B often   C never
  decorate the room?   A always   B often   C never

2 At your party do you …
  talk to your friends?   A always   B often   C never
  play music?   A always   B often   C never
  dance with your friends? A always   B often   C never

3 After the party do you …
  clean up?   A always   B often   C never

Mostly A answers	You always have great parties!
Mostly B answers	You often have good parties!
Mostly C answers	You don't like parties!

3 Talk about you and your friend.

Before my parties I often make the food. My friend never goes shopping.

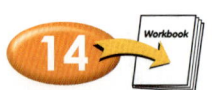

Unit 2 Lesson 4 — I Know...

1 Complete and learn.

Language Check

ALWAYS	NEVER	OFTEN
I _always drink_ _tea_ .	I _never drink_ _coffee_ .	I _often eat_ _cake_ .
She _____ _____ .	He _____ _____ .	She _____ _____ .
They _____ _____ .	They _____ _____ .	They _____ _____ .

2 Write.

1. hat / wears / he / never / a — He never wears a hat.
2. August / snows / never / it / in _____
3. I / up / always / get / six / at / o'clock _____
4. bike / you / your / often / ride _____
5. parties? / like / does / he _____
6. she / always / does / do / tricks? _____

Word Fun 3 Write the words in the puzzle.

1. Girls wear these to parties.   _ _ _ _ S
2. We wear this in school.   U _ _ _ _ _ _ _
3. You wear it to gym.   _ _ _ _ _ _ I _
4. Farmers wear these on their feet. _ _ _ _ T _

Unit 2 — Lesson 5

We're going to make a party invitation in school today.
We need **paper, markers,** and **crayons!**
Hooray, hooray, hooray!

1   carnival costume (n)   cowboy hat (n)
       Halloween costume (n)   pajamas (n)

2 Make your party invitation.

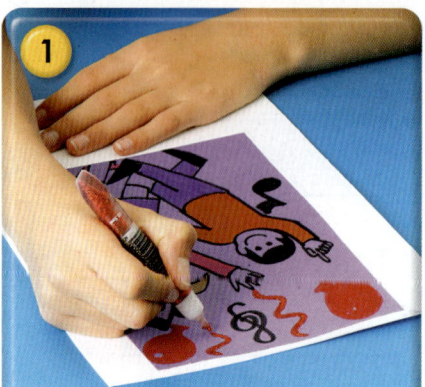

Draw a picture of a party at the top of the page. Leave space at the bottom for lines of writing.

At the bottom, write and draw lines with a black marker.

This is your invitation to my party

on _____

at _____

at _____

Please wear _____
_____

Then complete the invitation.

Line 1: Date.
Line 2: Address.
Line 3: Time.
Line 4: Choose the clothes, e.g. carnival costume, Halloween costume, cowboy hat, or pajamas!

3 Ask and answer.

When is your party?

On Saturday November 3rd.

Unit 2 Lesson 6

1 Look at the pictures and answer Yes or No.

1 eat an apple
   | Every day | Yes | Now | ___ |

2 eat candy
   | Every day | ___ | Now | ___ |

3 wear a school uniform
   | Every day | ___ | Now | ___ |

4 drink a soda
   | Every day | ___ | Now | ___ |

Every day

Now

Values!
Celebrating is fun!

2 Listen and read. Then sing.

It's My Birthday

I always do my homework.
I do my homework every day.
But now I'm playing games.
It's my birthday today.
Hooray, hooray, it's my birthday today.

I always read a book.
I read a book every day.
But now I'm reading comics.
It's my birthday today.
Hooray, hooray, it's my birthday today.

Unit 2 Lesson 7 — Science

1 hot (adj)　　cold (adj)　　wet (adj)　　dry (adj)

2 Listen and read. Then match the people and animals with the places.

Deserts are very dry. It doesn't often rain and the sun shines every day. It's always very hot in the day and very cold at night. It's often windy in deserts. People in deserts always wear long clothes and scarves around their heads. They walk or often ride camels.

It's always hot and wet in rain forests. It rains but it's often sunny. There are big trees, it can be dark. People in the rain forests always wear thin clothes. There are lots of monkeys, parrots, snakes, and spiders in rain forests.

3 Write the answers in your notebook.

1. Does it often rain in deserts?
2. What do the people always wear in rain forests?
3. What do the people often ride in deserts?

Unit 2 Lesson 8

Fantastic Fun!

Stone and Bone
Act it out!

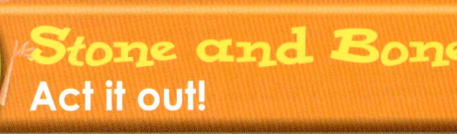

We always eat bread and honey for breakfast.

I never eat bread and honey. I always eat a big hamburger!

Dictation Time!

Listen and take notes.

	Number of letters	It begins with
1 A month	7	J
2 A day	__	__
3 A number	__	__
4 An animal	__	__

Now write the answers.

1 January
2 _____
3 _____
4 _____

My Writing

Connect the sentences with *but*.

1 He often reads books. He never reads comics.
   <u>He often reads books but he</u>
   <u>never reads comics.</u>

2 It's often windy. It's never cold.
   _____
   _____

Write the new words in your Fantastic Dictionary.

Workbook 19

The "Yes" Game

 **1** Listen and read.

2 **Write the answers in your notebook.**

1. What does Mike do every Monday?
2. What does Mike do every Saturday?
3. Does Mike like the "No" game?
4. Is Mike going to play the "Yes" game from now?
5. Do you play the "Yes" game or the "No" game with your parents?

3 **Act out a "No" game and a "Yes" game.**

Unit 3

Lesson 1

Look and Learn
She pick**ed** apples.
He tri**ed** to brush the horses.
She drop**ped** some eggs.

1 pick (v)   drop (v)   collect (v)   try (v)

2 Listen and read.

The Ranch
by Emma
Yesterday we worked on a ranch with Bob. What a day! Bob tried to brush the horses. I picked apples from the trees. Penny collected eggs from the ducks and the chickens. She dropped some eggs.

3 Underline the verbs in Activity 2.

4 Write the correct verb. Then say.

1 Yesterday morning I (pick) _____ some pears.

2 Yesterday you (drop) _____ some apples.

3 Yesterday afternoon she (collect) _____ some eggs.

4 Last week he (work) _____ on a ranch.

5 Last Friday they (try) _____ to brush a horse.

Say! What a day!

Unit 3 Lesson 2

Look and Learn

Sara didn't work.

1 Listen and read.

Our day on the ranch was great! Sam and I painted the ranch house. It was cool but the farmer didn't like the colors! Sara didn't work. She chased some ducks into the river.

2 Write T (true) or F (false).

1 Joe painted the farmer's car. F
2 The farmer didn't like the colors. ☐
3 Sam helped Bob. ☐
4 Sara chased a cow. ☐
5 The ducks jumped into the house. ☐

3 Correct the false sentences.

Joe didn't paint the farmer's car. He painted the farmer's house.

Unit 3 — Lesson 3

Look and Learn

Did you **work** all day?
No, we **didn't**.

What **did** you **do**?
I **fried** some eggs.

1 start (v)   stop (v)
   fry (v)   play (v)

2 Listen and read. Then act it out.

Did you work all day?

No, we didn't. We started at nine o'clock and stopped at two.

What did you do then?

I fried some eggs. Sam and Joe washed the walls. Emma dived in the river and played with the ducks! And Sara watched us!

3 Ask and answer.

Did Penny fry some eggs yesterday afternoon?

Yes, she did.

4 Listen and say.

Did the duck dive?

24

Unit 3 Lesson 4 — I Know...

1 Complete and learn.

Language Check

QUESTION	AFFIRMATIVE	NEGATIVE
What _did_ you _do_ ?	I play _ed_ the flute.	I _didn't play_ the violin.
What ___ he ___ ?	He climb___ a tree.	He _____ a wall.
What ___ she ___ ?	She wash___ her face.	She _____ her hair.
What ___ they ___ ?	They pick___ apples.	They _____ pears.

2 Complete the questions. Then write Yes, I did or No, I didn't.

1. you / wash your face / this morning?
   <u>Did you wash your face this morning?</u>   <u>Yes, I did.</u>

2. you / walk to school / this morning?
   _____ ?   _____

3. you / watch TV / last night?
   _____ ?   _____

Word Fun 3 Find the verbs in the banana tree!

1. <u>work</u>
2. _____
3. _____
4. _____
5. _____
6. _____

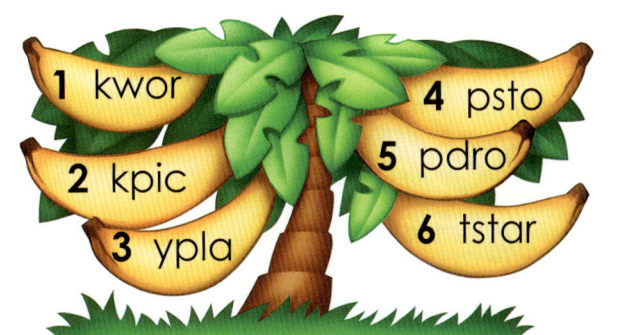

1 kwor
2 kpic
3 ypla
4 psto
5 pdro
6 tstar

Unit 3 — Lesson 5

We're going to make an animal chart in school today.
We need **paper, crayons,** and **scissors.**
Hooray, hooray, hooray!

1  wild animals (n)   farm and ranch animals (n)   pets (n)

2 Make an animal chart.

Draw an animal chart.

Draw a wild animal, a ranch animal, and a pet. Cut out your pictures.

Paste your picture in the correct circles.

3 Play "Guess the animal."

- This animal isn't a pet.
- Is it dangerous?
- Yes, it is.
- Is it a snake?
- Yes, it is.

Unit 3 Lesson 6

 **1** Listen and complete. Then sing the song.

In the Countryside

Yesterday we walked in a field with flowers.
In the countryside. In the countryside.
Did you pick the flowers?
Yes, we did. Yes, we did.
In the countryside. In the countryside.

Yesterday we walked on the hill near a lake.
In the countryside. In the countryside.
Did you dive in the lake?
It was great! _____
In the countryside. In the countryside.

Yesterday we walked in a field with sheep.
In the countryside. In the countryside.
Did you count the sheep?
And we fell asleep! _____
In the countryside. In the countryside.

2 Write the answers in your notebook.

1. Did the children walk in the town yesterday?
2. Did they pick apples yesterday?
3. Did they dive in the lake yesterday?
4. Did they walk in the fields?

Values!

Enjoy outdoor activities.

Unit 3 Lesson 7 History

1 sail (v)   arrive (v)   people (n)   land (n)

2 **Listen and read.**

Thanksgiving

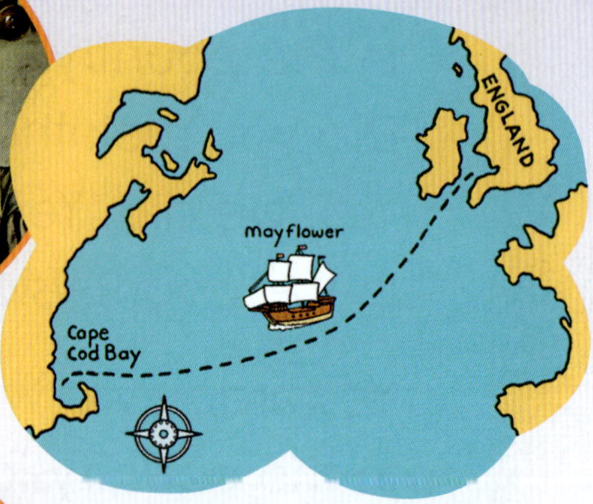

On September 8th, 1762, some people sailed from England to America in a small ship. The ship was the *Mayflower*. The people were Pilgrims.

The Pilgrims arrived in America. It rained and snowed, but the Pilgrims loved America. It was a beautiful country with fields, rivers, and lakes.

When spring arrived, there was lots of good food and the Pilgrims liked the Native Americans, the people of America. In the fall, there was a big party with the Native Americans and the Pilgrims. Now Americans have Thanksgiving dinners on the fourth Thursday in November. They thank friends and family for good food and their country.

3 **Write the story.**

The Pilgrims __sailed__ to America. They _____ in America. It rained and _____ . The Pilgrims _____ America and they _____ the Native Americans. In the fall, there _____ a big party with the Native Americans.

Unit 3 Lesson 8 — Fantastic Fun!

Stone and Bone
Act it out!

Did you pick some apples, Dina?

Yes, I did. Here you are!

Dictation Time!
Listen and number.

My Writing

Connect the sentences with *and then*.

1. She washed her face. She brushed her teeth.

   <u>She washed her face and then she brushed her teeth.</u>

2. He studied. He listened to music.

   _____

   _____

3. They arrived. They started work.

   _____

   _____

Write the new words in your Fantastic Dictionary.

Unit 4

Lesson 1

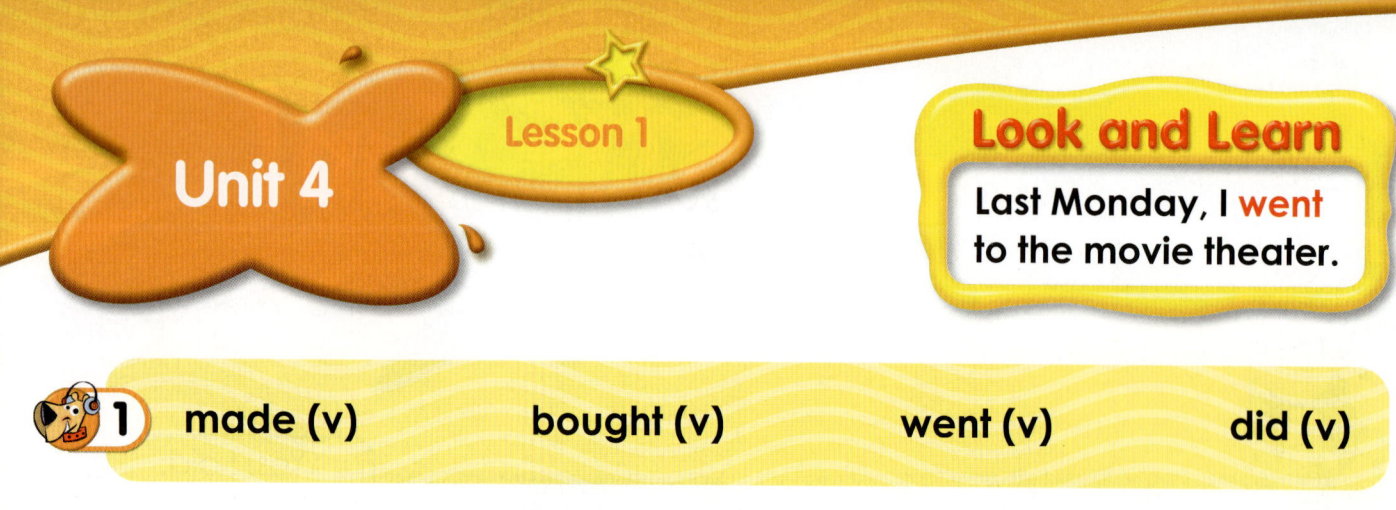

Look and Learn

Last Monday, I went to the movie theater.

1 made (v)   bought (v)   went (v)   did (v)

2 Listen and write the days.

3 Read and complete the sentences.

1 Last Sunday, Sara d<u>id</u> her homework.

2 Last Tuesday, Penny and Sara m_____ a cake.

3 Last Monday, Sara b_____ a dress.

4 Last Friday, Bob, Joe, and Sara w_____ to the movie theater.

5 Last Wednesday, Sara s_____ her grandma.

Unit 4 — Lesson 2

Look and Learn

Did you **go** to the movies **last week**?
Yes, we **did**.

1 Listen and read. Then act it out.

Friday

Thursday

Saturday

Did Sara buy a new dress on Saturday?

No, she didn't. She bought it on Monday.

Did you go to the movies last week?

Yes, we did. We went on Friday!

We saw a cowboy movie. It was great!

Say!

It was great!

2 Ask and answer.

1. have a party
2. go to school
3. make a cake
4. do your homework
5. go shopping
6. see a cowboy movie

Did you have a party last week?

No, I didn't.

Unit 4 — Lesson 3

1 weekend (n)   soccer (n)
softball (n)   sports stadium (n)

Look and Learn
What did Joe do last Sunday?
He brushed his dog.

2 Listen and say. Then play "the weekend game."

What did Joe do last Sunday?

He brushed his dog.

THE WEEKEND GAME

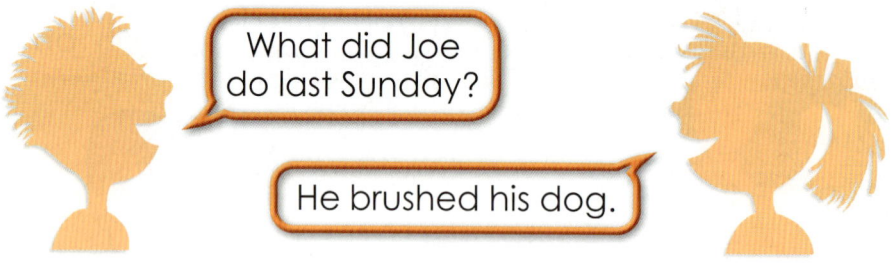

	SATURDAY	SUNDAY
Joe	did his homework	brushed his dog
Claire	bought a book	made a cake
Bob and Rick	watched television	played soccer
Sue	played softball	ran at the sports stadium

3 Write what Bob and Rick did last weekend in your notebook.

4 Listen and say.

buy   bought   catch   caught
Every day I teach.   Yesterday I taught.

Unit 4 Lesson 4 — I Know...

1 Complete and learn.

Language Check

QUESTION	NEGATIVE	AFFIRMATIVE
Did you _go_ to the movies?	No, we _didn't_ .	We _went_ to a party.
____ he/she _____ Eric?	No, he/she _____ .	He/She _____ Adam.
____ they _____ a cake?	No, they _____ .	They _____ a pizza.

2 Correct the sentences.

1. The boy went to the bookstore.
   <u>No, he didn't. He went to the clothes store.</u>

2. He bought a red jacket.
   _____

3. He had a salad for breakfast.
   _____

Word Fun 3 Write the past verbs in your notebook.

> do   stop   have   run   go   work   like   buy

REGULAR VERBS	IRREGULAR VERBS
stopped	had

Unit 4
Lesson 5

We're going to make a diary in school today.
We need **paper, crayons,** and **markers.**
Hooray, hooray, hooray!

 **1**   draw (v)   write (v)   read (v)   clean (v)

2 Make a diary for a week.

Draw lines to make a diary.

Write "My Week" and the days of the week.

Write what you did last week. Use drew, wrote, read, cleaned, etc.

3 Play a game.

Who drew a picture last week?

Jack did. He drew a picture last Wednesday.

1 Listen and complete. Then sing the song.

Aliens

It was _____ and _____ . It walked into the _____ .

And it jumped on the bed.

The alien danced around the _____ .

Then it walked down the stairs. It went into the _____ .

And sat on all the chairs. It ran into the kitchen.

It ate ham and two fried eggs.

Then it went into the _____ .

And painted the table legs.

2 Answer the questions.

1 Where did the alien jump?   It jumped on the bed._____

2 Where did the alien dance?   _____

3 Where did the alien run?   _____

4 What did the alien eat?   _____

5 Where did the alien sit?   _____

Unit 4 — Lesson 7

History

 **1** cave (n)   stone (n)   skin (n)   jewelry (n)

2 Read and complete.

eat   ~~live~~   paint   make   clean

Cave people

The first people didn't live in houses.
They ___lived___ in caves and they often
_____ pictures on the walls. There were always animals in their pictures.

The cave people _____ meat, fish, vegetables, and fruit. They didn't have knives, but they had stones.

They _____ the skins of the animals and made clothes from them. They often _____ jewelry from the teeth of the animals.

 **3 Listen and check your answers.**

4 Complete the table in your notebook.

CAVE PEOPLE			
House	Food	Clothes	Jewelry
caves			

Values!
Learn about your history.

Unit 4 Lesson 8

Fantastic Fun!

Stone and Bone
Act it out!

Here's a present for you, Bone.

Oh, thank you, Stone! It's beautiful. Did you make it?

Yes, Bone made it. But it was my tooth!

Dictation Time!

Listen and circle.

1 I read a story about a (bear) / pear.

2 I bought some flour / flowers.

3 I ate some bread and jam / ham.

4 I saw a very fat dog / duck.

5 I didn't see any paper / pepper.

My Writing

Connect the sentences with *and then*. Use *it*.

1 She washed her hair. She brushed her hair.

   She washed her hair and then she dried it.

2 They made a cake. They ate the cake.

   _____

   _____

Write the new words in your Fantastic Dictionary.

Reading Time

The Lion's Friend

1 Listen and read.

1. Bruno and Sophia lived on a farm. The farm was near a forest with wild animals. One day the children and their father heard Grrrr … Grrrr …

Grrrr … Grrrr …

2. In the cave there was a lion with a thorn in its foot. The children's father took the thorn out. The lion stood up and ran into the forest.

3. Two months later.
The children and their parents were on the farm. Then they heard Clip! Clop! It was a soldier on a horse. The soldier took Sophia's father to the town.

4. Bruno and Sophia went to the town.

Some men are going to fight wild animals here today.

Oh, no! That's our father with the lion.

38

The lion ran to their father, then stopped! Their father dropped his sword. Then their father and the lion walked from the circus ring. The people cheered and clapped.

Oh, Father! Are you OK?

I'm fine. That was the lion from the cave. We helped him and now he is a good friend.

2 Match.

Clip! Clop!   Oh, Father!   Oh, no!   Grrrr … Grrrr …

3 Write the story in the correct order.

The lion stopped.
The lion ran to the father.
The people cheered and clapped.
The father and the lion were in the circus ring.
The lion and the father walked from the circus ring.
The father dropped his sword.

<u>The father and the lion were in the circus ring.</u>
_____
_____
_____
_____

Unit 5

Lesson 1

Look and Learn
Millie is fast**er than** Minnie.

1 fast (adj) slow (adj) pretty (adj) young (adj)

2 Listen and read. Then act it out.

Joe has lots of pets! This is my favorite, Minnie! She's very pretty.

Oh, I think this mouse, Millie, is prettier.

Millie is younger and faster than Minnie, but she isn't prettier! I think she's ugly! Ouch! Look out! Her teeth are very big.

Say!
Look out!

3 Complete the sentences.

1 Millie ____is faster than____ Minnie. (fast)
2 Millie _____ Minnie. (young)
3 Millie _____ Minnie. (pretty)
4 Minnie _____ Millie. (slow)

Unit 5 Lesson 2

Look and Learn

Is Sid old**er than** her?

1 Listen and read. Then act it out.

Sally won the race! She's the champ! Sid is slower than Sally. Is Sid older than her?

Yes, he is. Sally's very young. She's only one year old and she's faster.

Say!

Sally won the race!

2 Answer the questions.

1. Is Sid slower than Sally?   Yes, he is.
2. Is Sid older than Sally?   _____
3. Is Sally younger than Sid?   _____
4. Is Sid faster than Sally?   _____

3 Ask and answer.

9   8   7

Is Emma older than Joe?

Yes, she is.

4 Listen and say.

Sid is slower than Sally.

Unit 5 Lesson 3

Look and Learn

The new coat is **more expensive than** the old coat.

1 colorful (adj)   expensive (adj)
beautiful (adj)   comfortable (adj)

2 Listen and read. Then act it out.

What are you doing, Sara?

I'm brushing your dog. He's more beautiful now. And I bought a coat for him. I think it's more colorful and more comfortable than his old coat. And it was more expensive!

3 Ask and answer.

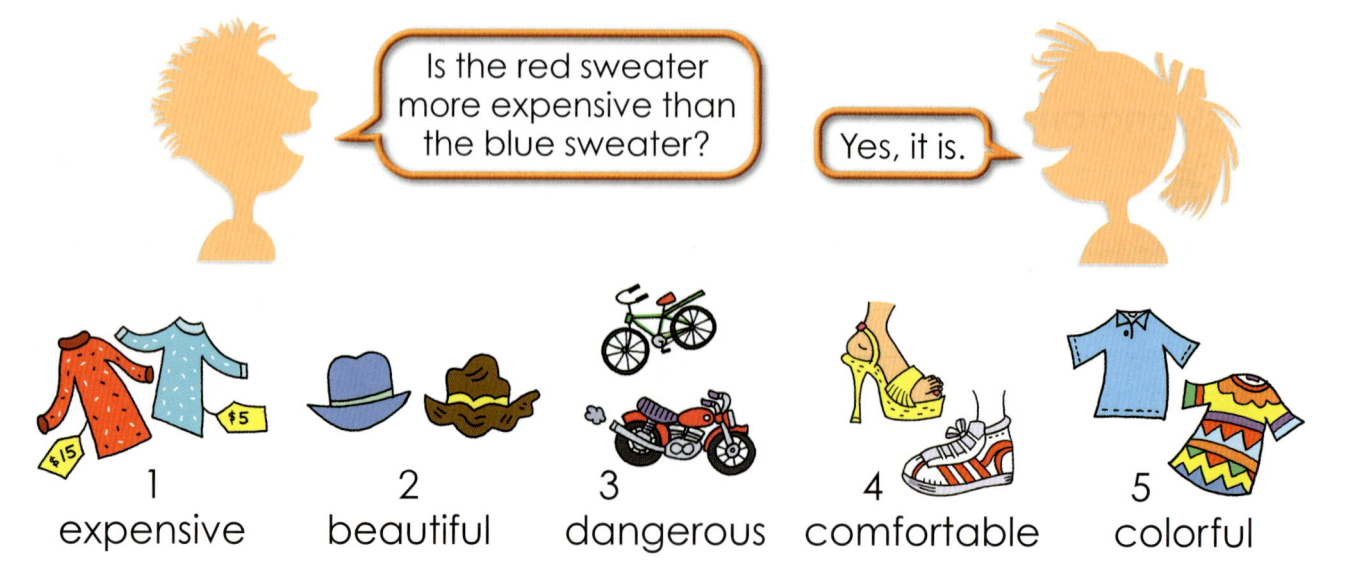

Is the red sweater more expensive than the blue sweater?

Yes, it is.

1 expensive
2 beautiful
3 dangerous
4 comfortable
5 colorful

Unit 5 Lesson 4 — I Know...

1 Complete and learn.

Language Check

long	fat	happy	colorful
longer	_fatter_	_happier_	_more colorful_
short	big	pretty	comfortable
_____	_____	_____	_____
young	hot	ugly	expensive
_____	_____	_____	_____

2 Complete the sentences.

1. Summer is hotter than winter.
   Winter _is colder than summer._

2. Mice are smaller than hamsters.
   Hamsters _____ .

3. Buses are slower than planes.
   Planes _____ .

Word Fun 3 Find and circle eight adjectives. Then write four sentences in your notebook.

E	B	I	G	F	A	S	T	S
X	O	L	D	A	Q	L	A	M
P	R	E	T	T	Y	O	L	A
E	Z	Q	X	U	O	W	L	L
N	L	O	N	G	U	Z	T	L

Workbook 43

Unit 5
Lesson 5

We're going to make a body chart in school today.
We need **paper, a tape measure,** and **markers.**
Hooray, hooray, hooray!

1   feet (n)   head (n)   body (n)   arms (n)

2   Make your body chart.

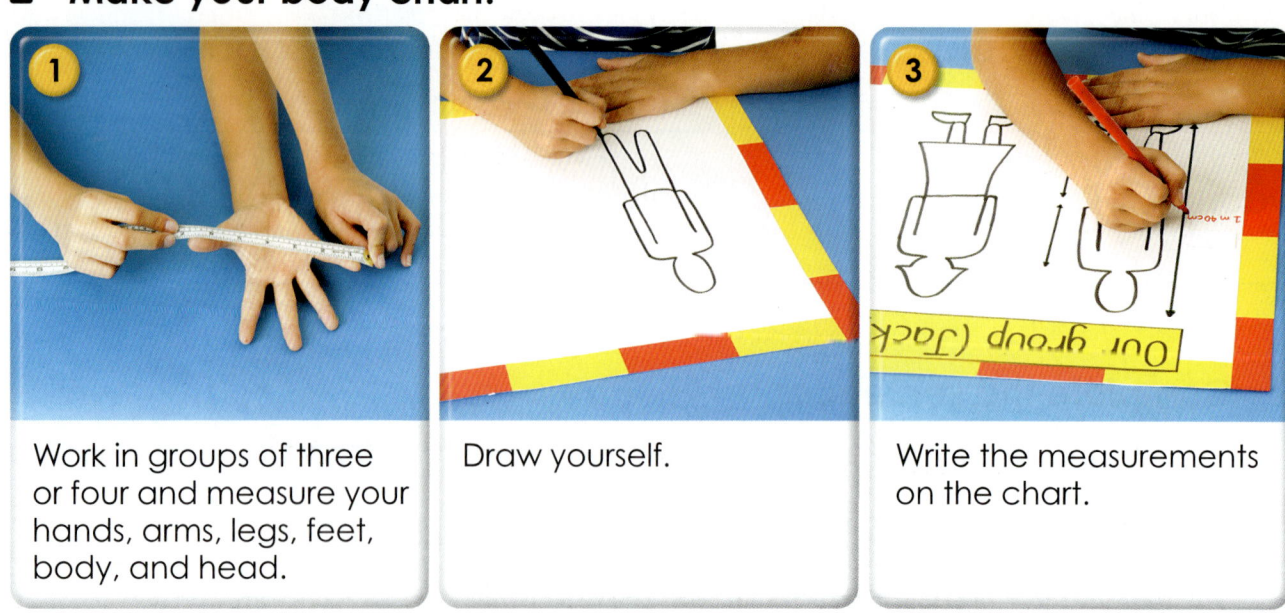

1. Work in groups of three or four and measure your hands, arms, legs, feet, body, and head.
2. Draw yourself.
3. Write the measurements on the chart.

3   Talk about your group.

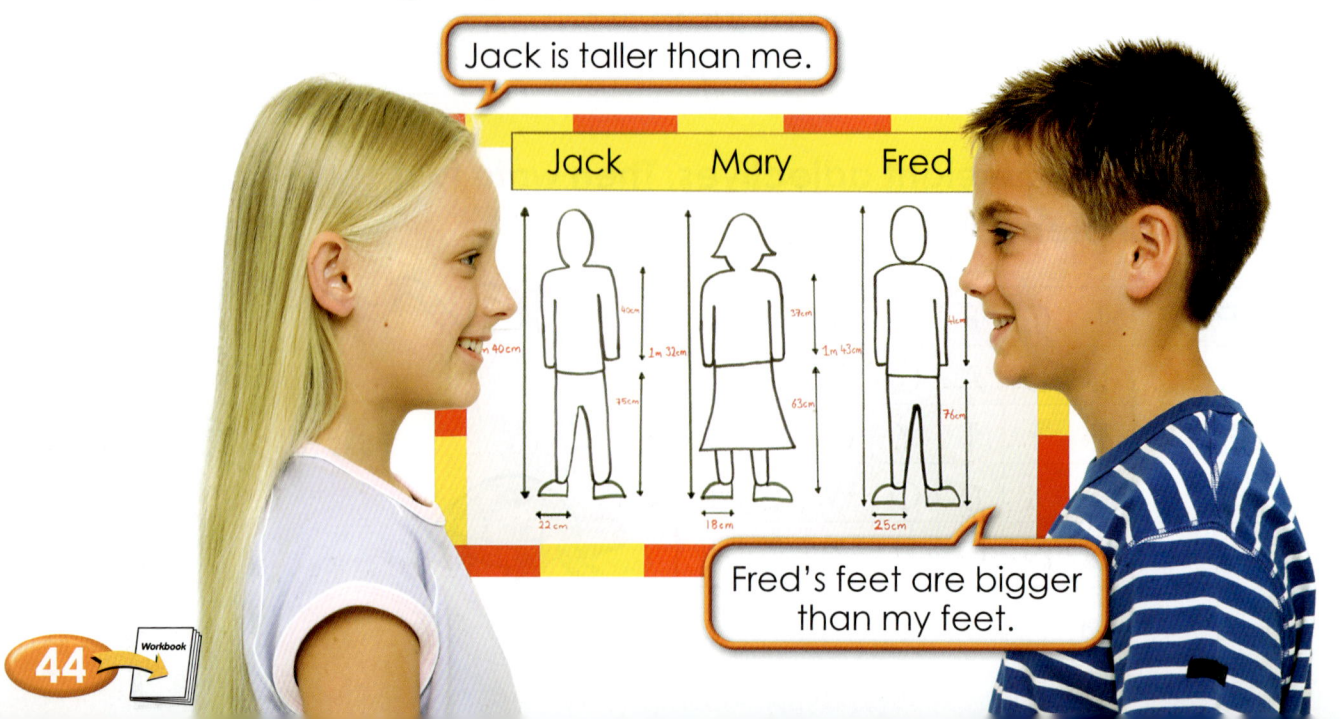

Jack is taller than me.

Fred's feet are bigger than my feet.

Unit 5 Lesson 6

1 Listen and complete. Then sing the song.

What's for Dinner?

It's _shorter_ than me.
And I can see
It's _____ than a dog
And it can't be a frog.
Is it a rabbit?
No, it's _____ .
Oh, I think it's a mouse.
Great! Let's have dinner!

It's _____ than me.
And I can see
It's _____ than a dog
And it can't be a frog.
Is it a rabbit?
No, it's _____ .
Oh, I think it's a cat.
Run! I'm not for dinner!

2 Write your song.

fat   tall   big   dangerous

It's _____ than me.
And I can see
It's _____ than a dog
And it can't be a frog.

Is it a rabbit?
No, it's _____ than a rabbit
And it's _____ than me.
I think it's a chimpanzee!

Unit 5 Lesson 7 Geography

1 cheetah (n)   chimpanzee (n)   panda (n)   giraffe (n)

2 Listen and write T (true) or F (false).

1. A cheetah is faster than a lion. ☐ T
2. A camel is taller than a giraffe. ☐
3. A panda has longer arms than a chimpanzee. ☐
4. A camel has thinner legs than a panda. ☐
5. An African elephant has bigger ears than an Indian elephant. ☐

cheetah
lion
Indian elephant
African elephant 
camel 
giraffe 
chimpanzee 
panda 

3 Make questions for the quiz. Then ask and answer.

WILD ANIMAL QUIZ

1. Is a cheetah faster than a lion?
2. Is _____ ?
3. Does _____ ?
4. Does _____ ?
5. Does _____ ?

Values!
Help to save wild animals.

Unit 5 Lesson 8
Fantastic Fun!

Stone and Bone
Act it out!

Oh, Bone! My friend Ty's bigger, taller, and faster than me.

But he isn't more beautiful than you, Dina!

Dictation Time!

Listen and circle.

1 That boy's (faster) / fatter than me.

2 That girl's taller / smaller than me.

3 Those shoes are more comfortable / more colorful than my shoes.

4 My sister's colder / older than you.

My Writing

Write the sentences with commas.

1 She's older taller and thinner than him.
   She's older, taller, and thinner than him.

2 This brown jacket is more beautiful more comfortable and more expensive than the gray jacket.

   _____
   _____
   _____

Write the new words in your Fantastic Dictionary.

Unit 6

Lesson 1

Look and Learn
I love wearing this costume.

1 Japan (n)   Spain (n)   India (n)   Russia (n)

2 Listen and read. Then act it out.

I love dancing to music from Spain.

I like wearing this costume from India, but I don't like carrying this toy elephant!

This costume is from Russia. I hate wearing this hat! I feel silly.

I love wearing this costume. It's from Japan. Sam loves dancing but he hates wearing his costume.

3 Write T (true) or F (false). Correct the false sentences in your notebook.

1. Penny hates wearing her costume.   F
2. Joe loves wearing his hat.
3. Emma likes wearing her costume.
4. Sam loves dancing.

Unit 6 Lesson 2

Look and Learn
Do you like painting?

1 Listen and read. Then act it out.

Around the world concert

Good job, Sara! Do you like painting those flags?

Yes, I do. I love drawing and painting. And I love having concerts.

Say!
Good job!

2 Ask and answer.
1 wearing costumes
2 painting pictures
3 having picnics
4 riding bikes

Do you like wearing costumes?

Yes, I do.

3 Listen and say.

I like riding a bike.

Unit 6 — Lesson 3

Look and Learn
Joe's **bad at** danc**ing**.

1
- good (adj)
- bad (adj)
- excellent (adj)
- terrible (adj)

2 Listen and read. Then chant.

Sara's good at painting.
Emma's good at running.
Bob's excellent at washing his old car.
Penny's bad at cooking.
Joe's bad at dancing.
Sam's terrible at playing his guitar!

3 Ask your friend and complete the chart.

	EXCELLENT	GOOD	BAD	TERRIBLE
dancing				
writing				
swimming				
cooking				

Are you good at dancing?

No, I'm not! I'm terrible at dancing.

4 Write about your friend.

My friend's excellent at reading. My friend's good at …

_____

_____

_____

Unit 6 — Lesson 4

I Know...

1 Write about you.

Language Check

I love listening to music.	I love _____ .
I like eating spaghetti.	I like _____ .
I don't like cleaning my room.	I don't like _____ .
I hate washing my hair.	I hate _____ .
I'm good at writing stories.	I'm good at _____ .
I'm bad at making cookies.	I'm bad at _____ .

2 Answer the questions.

1. Do you like going to school?   <u>Yes, I do!</u>
2. Are you good at learning English?   _____
3. Do you like doing your homework?   _____
4. Are you good at getting up in the morning?   _____

Word Fun 3 Write the –ing forms in the correct box in your notebook.

~~ride~~   ~~swim~~   ~~do~~   go   write   cut
drink   get   make   run   take   watch

WEAR → WEARING	DANCE → DANCING	SIT → SITTING
doing	riding	swimming

Workbook 51

Unit 6 · Lesson 5

We're going to make flags in school today.
We need **paper, markers,** and **crayons.**
Hooray, hooray, hooray!

1 Brazil (n)　the United States (n)　Germany (n)　Australia (n)

Argentina　Brazil　Canada　China　Germany　India　Italy

Japan　Mexico　New Zealand　Russia　Spain　the United States

2 Make a flag.

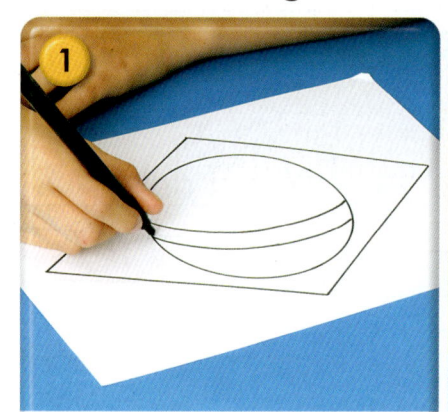

1. Draw a flag. 
2. Color the flag. 
3. Write a label for your flag and stick the flag on the wall.

3 Play a game.

Flags of the World

My flag is yellow, green, and blue.

No, it isn't.

Yes, it is.

Is it the flag of Spain?

Is it the flag of Brazil?

52　Workbook

Unit 6 Lesson 6

1 Listen and read. Then sing the song.

Friends Around the World

Friends around the world.
Friends around the world.
We're from Italy, China, and Russia,
And we're friends around the world.

We like meeting people.
We love having friends.
We like learning English
To talk to friends around the world.

Friends around the world.
Friends around the world.
We're from Brazil, Spain, and Japan,
And we're friends around the world.

2 Ask and answer.

Where are you from?

I'm from the United States.

Pleased to meet you!

Values!

Respect people around the world.

Unit 6, Lesson 7 — Geography

1 skiing (n)   hockey (n)   water-skiing (n)   rugby (n)

2 **Listen and read. Then complete.**

Canada

Canada is a big country with lakes and mountains. It always snows in the winter and it is very cold.

Many Canadians are good at skiing and skating. They often like playing or watching ice-hockey. The Canadian ice-hockey team is famous around the world.

New Zealand

New Zealand is a small __country__ with the ocean all around it. The sun often shines in New Zealand and it is _____ in the summer.

Many New Zealanders are good _____ swimming and water-skiing. They often like playing or watching rugby. The New Zealand rugby team is famous _____ the world.

3 Write about your country in your notebook.

_____ is a big / small country with _____ .

Unit 6 Lesson 8

Fantastic Fun!

Stone and Bone
Act it out!

Do you like painting, Stone?

Yes, I do.

Me too. But I'm not very good at it!

Dictation Time!

Listen and write L (like) or H (hate).

[L]   [ ]

[ ]   [ ]

[ ]   [ ]

My Writing

Connect the sentences with *or*.

1. I don't like writing letters. I don't like watching TV.

   I don't like writing letters or watching TV.

2. I don't like singing. I don't like dancing.

   _____

   _____

Write the new words in your *Fantastic Dictionary*.

Reading Time

The King of the Animals

1 Listen and read.
Then act out pictures 1, 2, and 3 of the story.

1.
Who is going to be king of the animals?
I am! I'm good at talking. I'm the best!

2.
I'm going to be king. I have strong teeth and my tail is very long.
Ha! Ha! Ha! You're small and weak. Kings are big and strong.

3.
I'm big and strong.
OK. You're our king.
Hooray! Hooray!

4.
The next day the elephant went for a walk in the jungle. There was a rope and the elephant's leg went in it.
I can help you Mr. Elephant!
You can't help me. You're small and weak.

The mouse climbed up the tree. He put his long tail around the tree. He cut the rope with his strong teeth.

The elephant told the story of the mouse to the animals. All the animals cheered and clapped. Next year the mouse is going to be king.

2 Circle.

strong teeth

good at talking

small and weak

big and strong

a long tail

3 Complete the elephant's story.

Yesterday I went for a ___walk___ in the jungle. My leg went in a _____ . The mouse saw me. The mouse _____ the tree. He _____ the rope with his strong _____ . I am the king now but next year the _____ is going to be _____ !

Unit 7

Lesson 1

Look and Learn
This baseball bat is **yours / mine / hers / his**.

1 skateboard (n)   baseball bat (n)   rollerblades (n)   skates (n)

2 Listen and read. Then act it out.

It's time to clean up. You kids are terrible! Let's clean this room. Emma, I think this baseball bat is yours.

Oh, yes! It's mine. And I think the skateboard is Sara's.

Oh, no! It isn't hers. It's Sam's. Oh, no! It isn't his. It's yours, Bob.

AFTER SCHOOL ADVENTURE CLUB

3 Complete the sentences.

1 Sam, here's your soccer ball. It's __yours__ .
2 It's Emma's baseball bat. It's _____ .
3 That's my skateboard. It's _____ .
4 These are Joe's shoes. They're _____ .

Say! It's time to clean up!

4 Say.

These are Joe's magazines. They're his.

1 JOE'S
2 Penny
3 SAM
4 Emma

Unit 7 — Lesson 2

Look and Learn

The skates are ours / theirs.

1 Listen and read. Then act it out.

Oh look, Sam! The rollerblades and the skates are ours.

And those books are mine! Check it out. There are rabbits in that box. They're Joe's, of course!

And I think these carrots are theirs!

2 Write and say.

1 My skates are old and Sam and Sara's skates are new. (theirs)
   My skates are old and theirs are new.

2 The rollerblades are Sam and Sara's. (theirs)
   _____

3 The magazines are mine and Joe's. (ours)
   _____

4 Penny's coat is green and mine and Emma's are blue. (ours)
   _____

3 Play a game.

Is this Mary's?

Yes, it is. It's hers.

No, it isn't. It's mine.

Unit 7 Lesson 3

Look and Learn

Whose book is this?
It's Penny's.
Whose rollerblades are these?
They're Sam and Sara's.

1 glasses (n)   eyes (n)
teeth (n)   legs (n)

2 Listen and read. Then play the game.

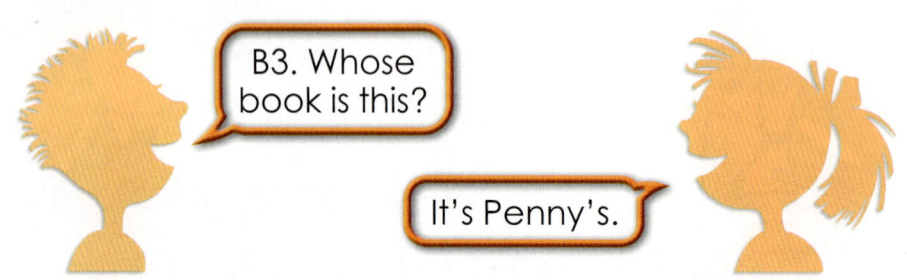

B3. Whose book is this?

It's Penny's.

3 Say and write.

1 That ball is ____Emma's____ .

2 Those magazines are _____ .

3 These cookies are the _____ .

4 Listen and say.

Whose shoes are these?

Unit 7 Lesson 4 — I Know...

1 Complete and learn.

Language Check

It's __my__ book.	It's mine.	They're my socks.	They're mine.
It's your pencil.	_____	They're _____ pens.	They're yours.
It's _____ car.	It's his.	They're his pants.	_____
It's her cup.	_____	They're _____ hats.	They're hers.
It's _____ tent.	It's ours.	They're our things.	_____
It's their video.	_____	They're _____ shoes.	They're theirs.

2 Write.

1 Whose recorder is this ? It's Al's.
2 _____ ? _____
3 _____ ? _____
4 _____ ? _____
5 _____ ? _____

Owen, Julia, Pete, Al, Mary

Word Fun 3 Write the words in the puzzle.

1 We wear these on our feet. S _ _ _ _ _
2 We go skating with these. _ K _ _ _ _ _
3 We play baseball with this. _ A _
4 We play tennis with this. _ _ _ _ _ T
5 We wear these to see. _ _ _ _ _ E _

Unit 7 Lesson 5

We're going to make a famous people poster in school today.
We need **scissors, paste, paper,** and **magazines.**
Hooray, hooray, hooray!

1 pop star (n)   movie star (n)   soccer player (n)   TV star (n)

2 Make a famous people poster.

1. Find a picture of your favorite famous person in a magazine. Cut out the picture. 
2. Write a heading for your poster. 
3. Paste your picture on a piece of paper and then put the poster on the wall.

3 Play a team game.

- Whose favorite famous person is this?
- Mark's.
- Who's this? He's a pop star.
- It's Sam Starr.
- Correct! Two points for team B.

62

Unit 7 — Lesson 6

1 Label the kitten.

- head
- body

2 Read and number the pictures in the correct order.

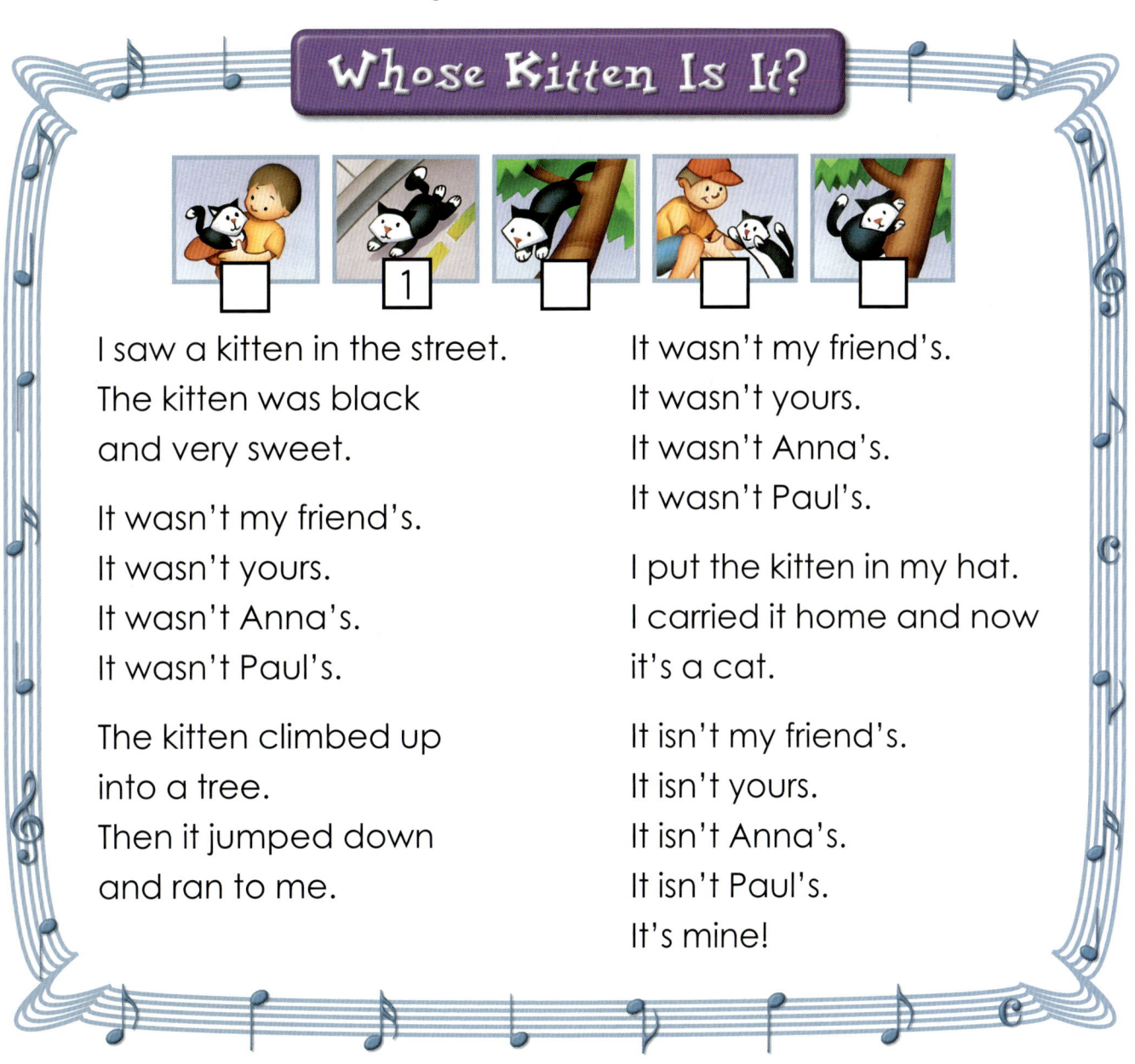

Whose Kitten Is It?

I saw a kitten in the street.
The kitten was black
and very sweet.

It wasn't my friend's.
It wasn't yours.
It wasn't Anna's.
It wasn't Paul's.

The kitten climbed up
into a tree.
Then it jumped down
and ran to me.

It wasn't my friend's.
It wasn't yours.
It wasn't Anna's.
It wasn't Paul's.

I put the kitten in my hat.
I carried it home and now
it's a cat.

It isn't my friend's.
It isn't yours.
It isn't Anna's.
It isn't Paul's.
It's mine!

3 Listen and sing the song.

Unit 7 · Lesson 7

Social Studies

1 cousin (n)   aunt (n)   uncle (n)   family (n)

2 **Listen and read.**

Families

There are big and small families. All families are different.

Look at Julie's family tree. She has a brother, a mom and a dad, and a grandma and grandpa. Julie's dad has a brother. He's Julie's uncle. Julie has an aunt, too. Her uncle and aunt have children and these are Julie's cousins.

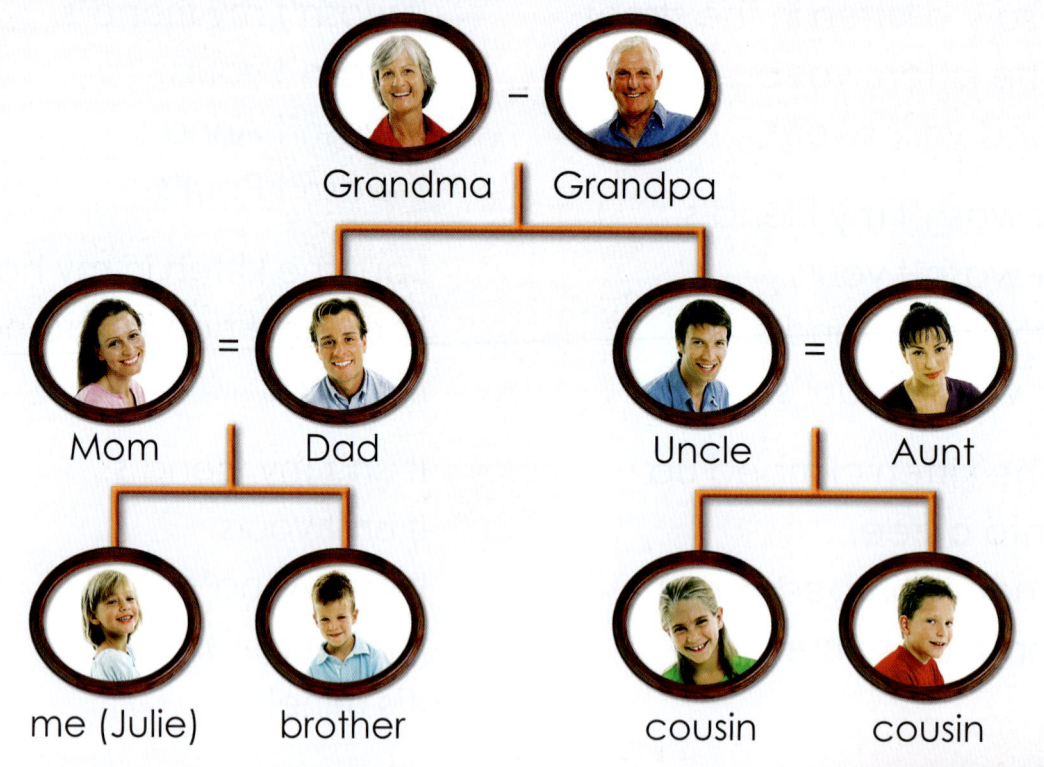

Grandma – Grandpa

Mom = Dad   Uncle = Aunt

me (Julie)   brother   cousin   cousin

3 Draw your family tree.

Values! Love your family.

Unit 7 Lesson 8

Fantastic Fun!

Stone and Bone
Act it out!

Whose glasses are these, Stone? Are they yours?

No, they aren't mine!

They're Dina's.

Dictation Time!

Listen and connect.

My Writing

Put in the apostrophes.

1 It's the boys and they're the girls.
   <u>It's the boy's and they're the</u>
   <u>girl's.</u>

2 The backpack isn't mine. It's that boys.
   _____
   _____

3 They aren't my glasses. They're Johns.
   _____
   _____

Write the new words in your Fantastic Dictionary.

Unit 8

Lesson 1

Look and Learn

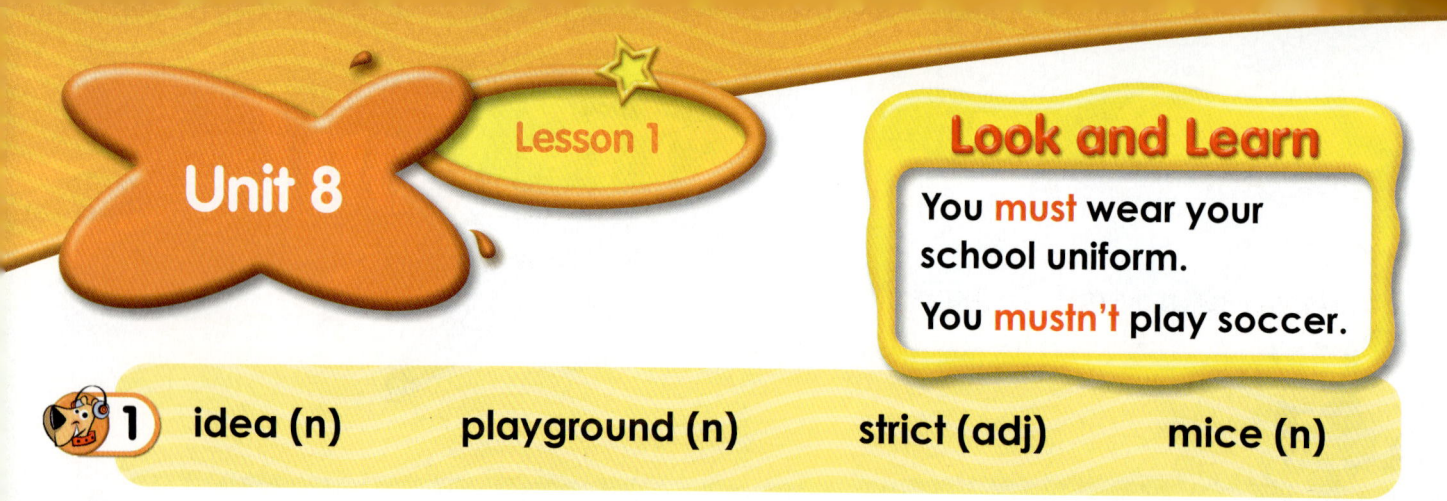

You **must** wear your school uniform.
You **mustn't** play soccer.

1 idea (n)   playground (n)   strict (adj)   mice (n)

2 Listen and read. Then act it out.

> Sara! You mustn't play soccer in the schoolyard. And you must wear your school uniform.

> That's the new teacher. She's very strict.

> And she doesn't like mice. I have an idea. It's funny!

3 Say and write.

1 Clean your desk!   You must clean your desk.
2 Don't touch that dog!   You mustn't touch that dog.
3 Write with a pen!   _____
4 Don't run!   _____
5 Don't jump on the desk! _____

Unit 8 Lesson 2

Look and Learn
What does she look like?

1 Listen and read. Then act it out.

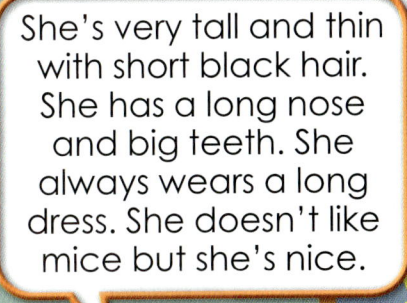

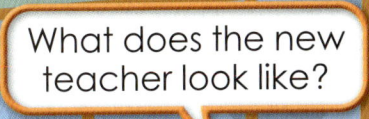

What does the new teacher look like?

She's very tall and thin with short black hair. She has a long nose and big teeth. She always wears a long dress. She doesn't like mice but she's nice.

Say!
She's nice.

2 Ask and answer.

- Sara
- Joe
- Penny
- Joe's mice

What does Sara look like?

She's pretty ...

3 Write about yourself.

What do you look like?

I'm _____

_____

_____

Unit 8 — Lesson 3

Look and Learn

She's **better at** math.
She's **the best** in the class.

1 English (n)　math (n)
　history (n)　geography (n)

2 Listen and read. Then chant.

Emma's good at English
But she's better at math.
She loves geography.
She's the best in the class!

Joe's bad at English
And he's worse at math.
He hates geography.
He's the worst in the class!

Report Card: Emma
English　8/10
Math　9/10
History　6/10
Geography　10/10

3 Look at the report cards and complete.

Emma is ___better___ at English than Joe.

Joe is ___worse___ at geography than math.

Joe is ___the worst___ at geography in the class.

Emma is _____ at geography than Joe.

Joe is _____ at English than math.

Joe is _____ at history in the class.

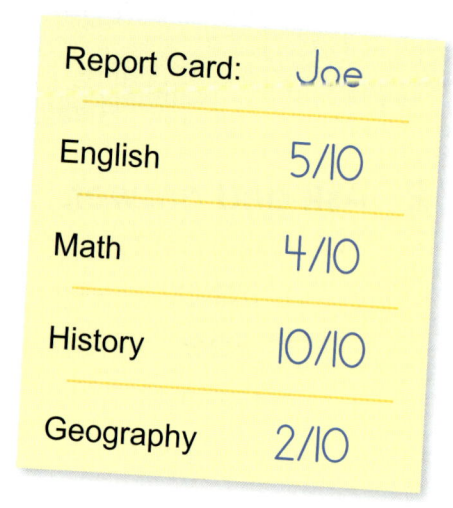

Report Card: Joe
English　5/10
Math　4/10
History　10/10
Geography　2/10

4 Listen and say.

He's the **w**orst **w**orker in the **w**orld.

Unit 8 Lesson 4

I Know...

1 Complete and learn.

Language Check		
good	_____	the best
bad	worse	the _____

2 Write about you and your classmates.

1 What must you do in class?

_____

2 What mustn't you do in class?

_____

3 What does your best friend look like?

_____

4 Who's the best at math in the class?

_____

5 What's your worst subject?

_____

Word Fun 3 Write the words in the correct box in your notebook.

~~count~~   ~~river~~   ~~date~~   ~~word~~   country   ruler
alphabet   old   verb   year   dictionary   triangle
world   cave   mountain   number

ENGLISH	MATH	HISTORY	GEOGRAPHY
word	count	date	river

Workbook 69

Unit 8 Lesson 5

We're going to make a schedule in school today.
We need **paper** and **crayons**.
Hooray, hooray, hooray!

1 art (n)   science (n)   physical education (n)   music (n)

2 Make a schedule.

1. Draw lines and divide the page into three columns and six rows. Write "Days," "Classes," and "I must" at the top of each column, and in each row write the school days.

2. In the second column write a class you have for every day.

3. Write the things you must take with you in the third column.

3 Tell your class about your best day, your worst day, and what you must take with you.

My best day is Wednesday. On Wednesdays I must take my gym clothes to school. My worst day is …

Unit 8 Lesson 6

1 Read and complete.

At School

At nine o'clock on Monday my classes start.

The first class is ___math___

and then we have _____ .

Then we have _____ .

Then we have a break.

I always have a drink.

I sometimes have a piece of cake.

The fourth class is _____

and then it's one o'clock.

Then it's _____ and _____

_____ .

And then the classes stop.

Monday	
9:00	Math Art English
	BREAK
12:00	History Music Physical Education

2 Listen and check your answers. Then sing the song.

3 Compare the schedule in Activity 1 with your schedule.

We don't start school at nine o'clock.
We start at …

Our first class isn't math.
It's …

Unit 8 Lesson 7

Social Studies

1 modern (adj)　　slippers (n)　　special (adj)　　ballet (n)

2 **Listen and read.**

Schools Around the World

What do the schools look like in Japan? They're usually modern and they're very clean. Every morning the students must clean their classrooms. They sweep the classroom floor and wash the windows. Japanese students must wear slippers in the classroom. They mustn't wear their shoes.

In the United States there are special schools for ballet dancing. The students have ballet lessons every day, but they have regular classes too. The students must do their homework for their regular classes and they must practice ballet for three hours every day. School starts at eight o'clock in the morning and finishes at seven o'clock in the evening!

3 **Write the answers in your notebook.**

1. What must the students in ballet schools do every day?
2. What must Japanese students do every day?

Values!
Follow school rules.

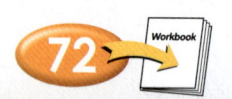

Unit 8 Lesson 8 — Fantastic Fun!

Stone and Bone
Act it out!

> Your teeth are very yellow, Dina. You must brush them every day!

> Here's a toothbrush for you.

Dictation Time!

Listen and number.

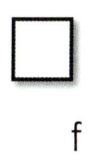

- a ☐
- b ☐
- c ☐
- d ☐ (1)
- e ☐
- f ☐

My Writing

Connect the sentences with *must* and *before*.

1. Wash your hands. Then you can eat.

   You <u>must</u> wash your hands <u>before</u> you eat.

2. Clean the classroom. Then you can play.

   _____

   _____

   _____

Write the new words in your Fantastic Dictionary.

Reading Time

The Unhappy Ghost

1 Listen and read. Then act it out.

1. Gonny was a ghost and he lived in a big house. Every night Gonny flew around the house. But Gonny wasn't a happy ghost. He didn't have any brothers, sisters, or friends.

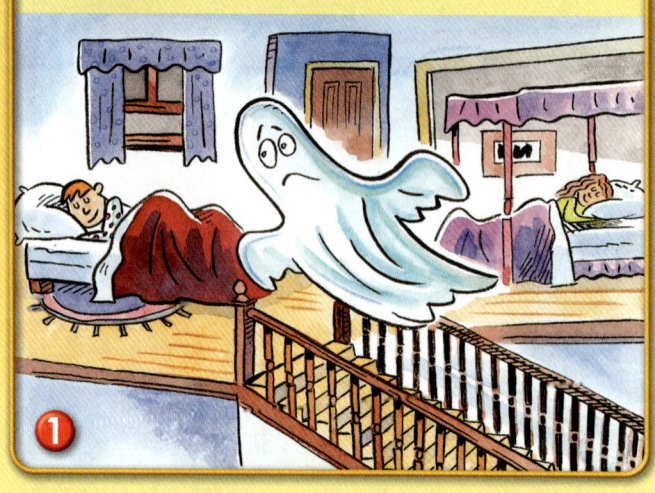

2. Two children lived in the house. Their names were Sally and Scott. Gonny liked them a lot. They went to school every day and Gonny often played with their skateboard.

3. One day it was Halloween. Sally was a witch and she had a tall black hat and a black dress. Scott was a wizard and he had a tall blue hat and a cloak.

"I don't have a wand."
"Here! You must have a wand."

4. "Wow! What a great costume!"
"Costume?"
"Yes. That's the best ghost costume in the world. You look like a ghost!"

Who are you?
I'm Gonny.
Oh, you're new here! Do you live near us?
Yes, very near!

Gonny was very happy. Now he had friends.
Come on! Let's go to the Halloween party.
I don't have an invitation.
But you gave the wand to us. You're our friend now.

2 Check ✓ the correct box.

Who …

1 … lived in a big house?

2 … wasn't happy?

3 … went to school every day?

4 … didn't have a wand?

5 … didn't have an invitation?

6 … went to the Halloween party?

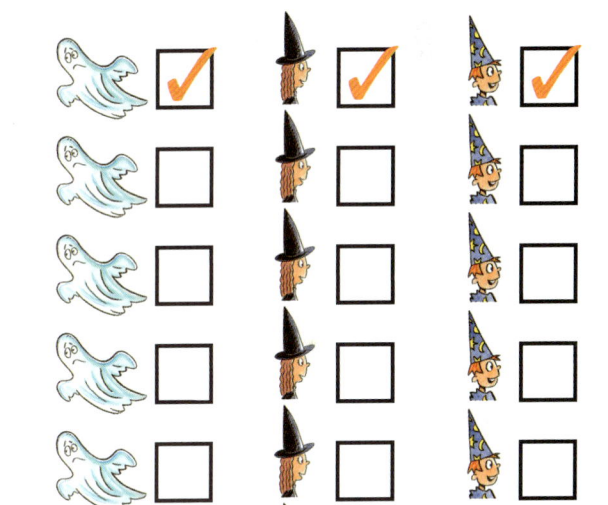

3 Match from the story.

happy — dress
tall — party
Halloween — ghost
black — hat

a b c d

Unit 9

Lesson 1

Look and Learn

There's **too much** wood.
There are **too many** nails.

1 dog house (n)　　wood (n)　　nails (n)　　screws (n)

2 Listen and read. Then act it out.

- We need some wood and some nails.
- Look! I think there's too much wood and there are too many nails.
- It doesn't matter. Joe's dog is very big!

3 Talk about the pictures.

- There's too much glue.
- There are too many ...

4 Write sentences in your notebook.

1 There __'s too much__ honey.　　2 There __are too many__ apples.

3 There / juice.　　4 There / nails.

5 There / glue.

Unit 9 Lesson 2

Look and Learn
There aren't **enough** screws.
There isn't **enough** paint.

1 Listen and read. Then act it out.

Now I need screws! Oh, no! I only have one. There aren't enough screws. What about the paint?

Here you are. There are more screws here, but there isn't enough paint.

Say!
Here you are.

2 Ask and answer.

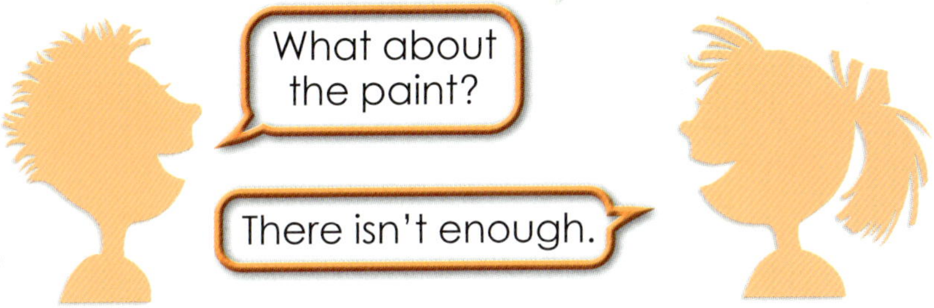

1 2 3 4 5

What about the paint?

There isn't enough.

3 Write.

There isn't enough juice.

Unit 9 Lesson 3

Look and Learn

How much milk is there?
How many socks are there?

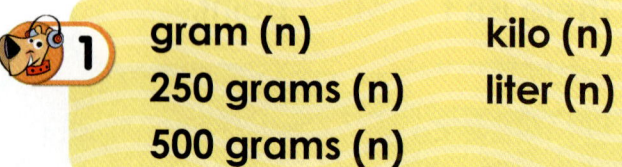

1
gram (n)   kilo (n)
250 grams (n)   liter (n)
500 grams (n)

2 Listen and play the game.

How much soda is there? — Two liters.
How many socks are there? — Ten.

3 Write the questions and answers.

How many hats are there? — Two.

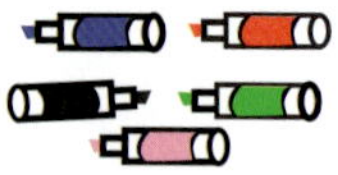

_____ _____

_____ _____

_____ _____

_____ _____

4 Listen and say.

A piece of cheese, please, Louise!

Unit 9 Lesson 4   # I Know...

1 Complete and learn.

Language Check

There are too many apples.	There's too much butter.
_____ pears.	_____ sugar.
There aren't enough apples.	There isn't enough butter.
_____ pears.	_____ sugar.
How many apples are there ?	How much butter is there ?
_____ pears _____ ?	_____ sugar _____ ?

2 Write the sentences in your notebook.

1. sugar / eggs
   There's too much sugar, but there aren't enough eggs.

2. people / food
   There are too many people, but there isn't enough food.

3. paint / wood   4 nails / screws   5 pens / paper

Word Fun 3 Write the words with a plural in A and the words without a plural in B.

salt   cookie   oil   orange   egg   ketchup
milk   hamburger

A

B

Unit 9 — Lesson 5

We're going to make a grocery store in school today.
We need **magazines, scissors, paper,** and **glue.**
Hooray, hooray, hooray!

1
a bag (n)   a bottle (n)   a can (n)   a jar (n)

2 Make a grocery store.

1. Cut out pictures of food from magazines. Find pictures of bags of cookies, bottles of juice, cans of soup, jars of peanut butter, etc.

2. Write "The Fantastic Grocery Store" on your paper.

3. Stick your pictures on the paper.

3 Act it out.

- Good morning.
- Good morning. Can I have two cans of soda, a bag of cookies, some cheese, and some oranges, please?
- How much cheese do you want?
- 250 grams of cheese, please.
- How many oranges do you want?
- Two kilos of oranges, please.

Unit 9 Lesson 6

1 Write the labels.

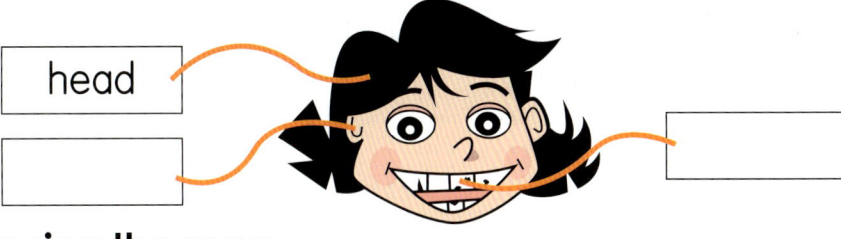

head

2 Listen and read. Then sing the song.

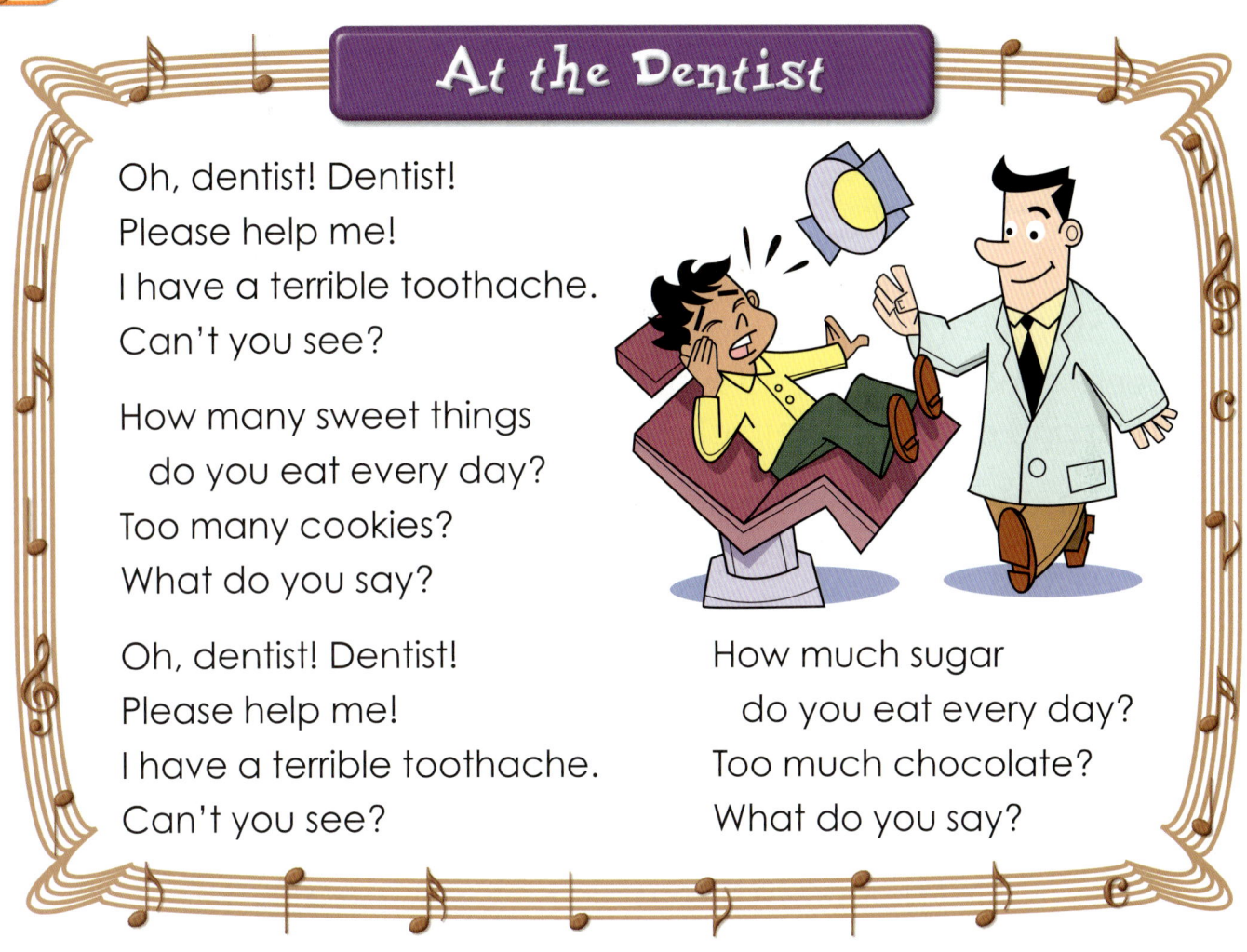

At the Dentist

Oh, dentist! Dentist!
Please help me!
I have a terrible toothache.
Can't you see?

How many sweet things
   do you eat every day?
Too many cookies?
What do you say?

Oh, dentist! Dentist!
Please help me!
I have a terrible toothache.
Can't you see?

How much sugar
   do you eat every day?
Too much chocolate?
What do you say?

3 Complete. Then say.

I have a terrible head____.

I have a terrible ear____.

Unit 9 Lesson 7

Social Studies

1   grow (v)   lose (v)   bite (v)   chew (v)

2 **Listen and read.**

At first young babies drink milk and then their teeth grow, and they can eat food. The first teeth are baby teeth. There are twenty baby teeth.

At about the age of six we lose our baby teeth and then our second set of teeth start to grow. There are thirty-two teeth in our second set. We need teeth to eat. Our front teeth bite our food and our back teeth chew it.

This boy doesn't have enough teeth.
He only has ten teeth from his second set.

But this girl has too many teeth!
Some people have extra teeth!

For healthy teeth you mustn't eat too much candy. You must brush your teeth every day. You don't need too much toothpaste, but you need a good toothbrush.

3 **Write the answers in your notebook.**

1 How many baby teeth do we have?

2 How many teeth do we usually have in our second set?

3 What must you do for healthy teeth?

4 What mustn't you do for healthy teeth?

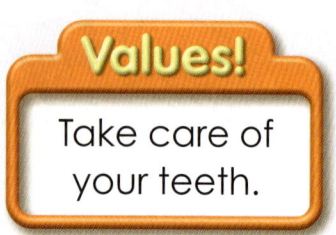

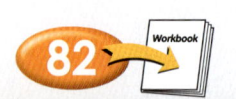

Values!
Take care of your teeth.

Unit 9 Lesson 8

Fantastic Fun!

Stone and Bone
Act it out!

I'm making a cake for Ty. How many eggs are there?

Not many. Only two.

Oh dear!

But they're very big eggs!

Dictation Time!

Listen and number.

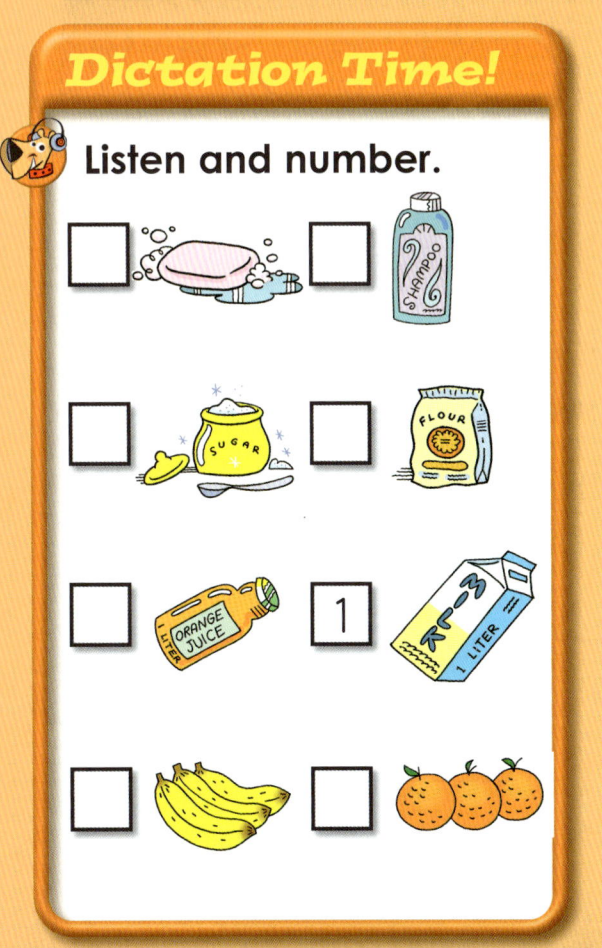

My Writing

Connect the sentences with *first* and *and then*.

1. Glue the wood. Nail the wood.
   <u>First glue the wood and then nail it.</u>

2. Nail the wood. Paint the wood.
   _____
   _____

3. Wash the pears. Cut the pears.
   _____
   _____

Write the new words in your Fantastic Dictionary.

Unit 10

Lesson 1

Look and Learn
Why don't we go water-skiing?

1 windsurfing (n)   ice-cream cone (n)   money (n)   home (n)

2 Listen and read. Then act it out.

- Let's go windsurfing!
- It's boring! Why don't we have an ice-cream cone?
- We don't have enough money! Why don't we go water-skiing?
- The water's cold. Why don't we go home!

3 Ask and answer.

1 2 3 4

Why don't we watch TV?

The shows are terrible.

4 Write the questions.

1 Let's go water-skiing!
   Why don't we go water-skiing?

2 Let's have a soda!
   _____

3 Let's dive in the ocean!
   _____

4 Let's play a game!
   _____

Unit 10 — Lesson 2

Look and Learn

I **could** swim last year, but I **couldn't** dive.

1 Listen and read. Then act it out.

I could swim last year, but I couldn't dive! Can you dive, Emma?

Yes, I can. I couldn't swim last year, but I'm a great swimmer now. I love swimming. It's so much fun!

Say!

It's so much fun!

2 Listen and mark ✓ or ✗.

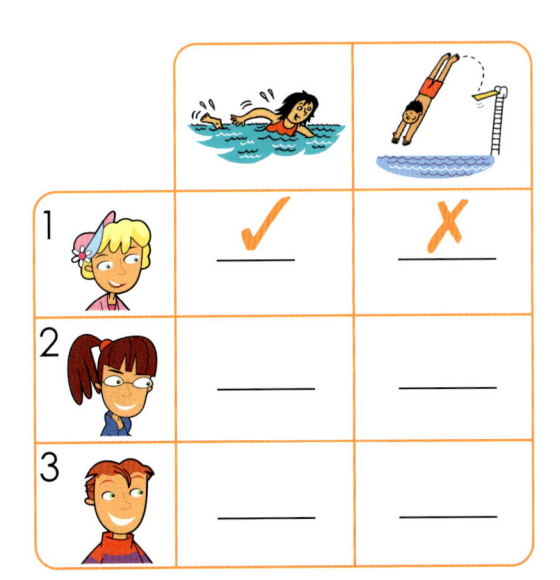

	🏊	🤿
1	✓	✗
2	___	___
3	___	___

3 Write sentences about Activity 2.

1 Sara could swim last summer, but she couldn't dive.

2 _____

3 _____

Unit 10 Lesson 3

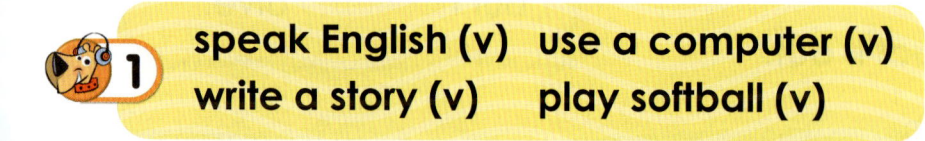

1 speak English (v)   use a computer (v)
write a story (v)   play softball (v)

Look and Learn

Could you ride a bike when you were seven?

2 Ask and answer.

Could you ... when you were seven?

	You	Your friend
1 ride a bike	✓	
2 make a cake		
3 write a story		
4 speak English		
5 use a computer		
6 play softball		

Could you ride a bike?

Yes, I could.

3 Say.

When I was seven I couldn't ride a bike, but my friend could.

4 Listen and say.

Jake makes cakes every day.

Unit 10 Lesson 4

I Know...

1 Complete and learn.

Language Check

QUESTION	AFFIRMATIVE	NEGATIVE
Could he write when he was four?	He _could_ walk.	He _couldn't_ read.
_____ they run when they were three?	They _____ walk.	They _____ sing.

2 Write the questions and answers.

1 Could you climb a tree when you were four?   No, I couldn't.

2 _____ when you were five?   _____

3 _____ when you were four?   _____

3 Complete the questions.

1 Why don't we go _windsurfing_ ?

2 Why don't we go _____ ?

3 Why don't we go _____ ?

Workbook 87

Unit 10 Lesson 5

We're going to make an action game in school today.
We need paper, paste, crayons, and markers.
Hooray, hooray, hooray!

1 play chess (v) ride a horse (v) catch a fish (v) make the bed (v)

2 Make an action game.

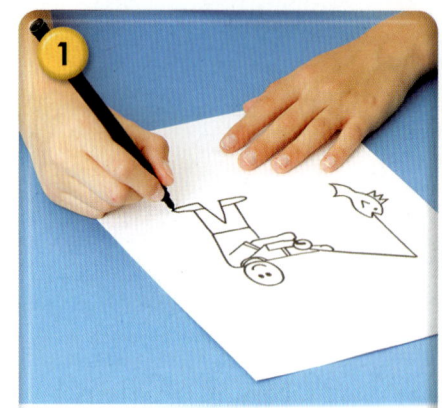

1. Draw a picture of a boy or girl doing an action – running, playing a guitar, etc. 
2. Paste all your pictures on a poster. 
3. Write labels for "Now," "Everyday," "Yesterday," and "Next week."

3 Play the action game.

What did he do yesterday?

He caught a fish.

now
every day
yesterday
next week

Unit 10 — Lesson 6

1 Match. Then listen and point.

1. turn around
2. jump
3. run
4. dance
5. walk
6. stamp your feet

2 Listen and read.

Move Around!

Yesterday I ran to school.
I often run. Running is cool.
Tomorrow I'm going to run to school.
And now I'm running. Running is cool.

Jump, dance, turn around.
Stamp your feet on the ground.
Jump, dance, turn around.
Stamp your feet. Move around.

Yesterday I walked to school.
I often walk. Walking is cool.
Tomorrow I'm going to walk to school.
And now I'm walking. Walking is cool.

Jump, dance, turn around.
Stamp your feet on the ground.

3 Now sing the song and perform the actions.

Unit 10 — Lesson 7

Science

1 crawl (v)   walk sideways (v)   slide (v)   climb (v)

2 Listen and read. Then answer.

Ocean animals

Crabs crawl on the rocks and walk sideways! They carry their home, their shell, with them. They have small eyes and eight legs.

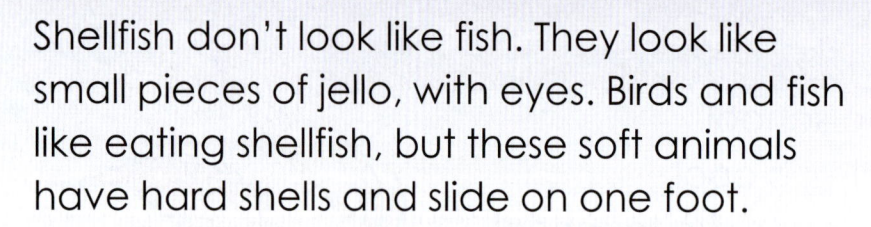

Shellfish don't look like fish. They look like small pieces of jello, with eyes. Birds and fish like eating shellfish, but these soft animals have hard shells and slide on one foot.

Starfish don't look like fish. Their body and five arms look like stars. They don't have eyes. They can't swim but they can climb rocks and crawl.

Which ocean animal slides on one foot? _____

Which ocean animal crawls and can't swim? _____

Which ocean animal walks sideways? _____

3 Complete.

	EYES	ARMS	LEGS	FEET	SHELL
CRAB	2	x	8	x	1
SHELLFISH					
STARFISH					

Values! Protect ocean animals.

Unit 10 Lesson 8

Fantastic Fun!

Stone and Bone
Act it out!

Look! I can stand on my head!

I could stand on my head at two!

I couldn't stand on my head at two! And I can't now!

Dictation Time!

Listen and write *yes* or *no*.

yes   no   ___   ___

___   ___   ___   ___

___   ___

My Writing

Write the sentences with *and*, *but*, or *or*.

1. I could walk. I could talk.

   I could walk and talk.

2. I could swim. I couldn't dive.

   _____

3. I couldn't read. I couldn't write.

   _____

4. I could draw. I couldn't paint.

   _____

Write the new words in your *Fantastic Dictionary*.

Reading Time

The Rich King

1 Listen and read.

1. There was a king. He had a pretty wife and two children. He lived in a big palace with a beautiful garden. But the king was a silly man.

"I have a lot of money. But I want to be richer!"

"Touch the apple!"

2. The king touched the apple and it changed to gold. Then he touched all the fruit, flowers, and trees in the garden and they changed to gold too.

3. The king was hungry and thirsty. He touched his food. It changed to gold. He touched his glass of water. It changed to gold. He couldn't eat or drink.

4. Then the king's wife and children ran into the room. The king touched them and they changed to gold.

> You had a beautiful wife and children. You could eat and drink and walk in your beautiful garden. But you wanted to be richer!

Please help me!

⑤

The wizard waved his wand and the king's garden, food, and family changed back.

> Thank you. I was a silly man! But now I'm happy.

⑥

2 Number the pictures in the correct order.

The king touched …

| | | 1 | | | | | |

… and they changed into gold.

3 Answer the questions.

1 Did the king have a lot of money? _____

2 Did he have an ugly wife? _____

3 Did he have three children? _____

4 Did he have a beautiful garden? _____

5 Did he want to be richer? _____

6 Was the king a silly man? _____

English is Fantastic!

1 Write all the phrases you can say.

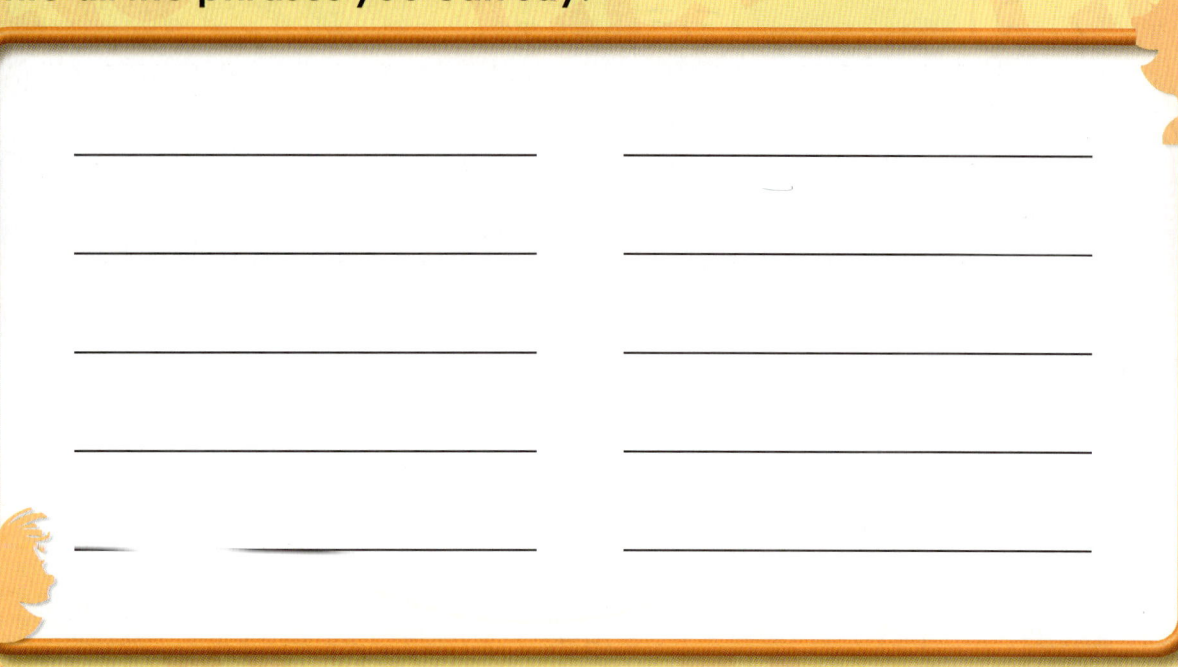

2 Write the words of your favorite song.

3 Write a description of your favorite *Reading Time* character.

_____
_____
_____
_____
_____
_____
_____

4 Paste your picture and write.

Fantastic!

Passport

Paste your picture here.

Name: _____

Nationality: _____

Best friend: _____

Age: _____

Congratulations

Put your fingerprint here.

Macmillan Education
Between Towns Road, Oxford OX4 3PP
A division of Macmillan Publishers Limited
Companies and representatives throughout the world

Student's Book pack ISBN-13 : 978-1-4050-7364-6
Includes:
Student's Audio CD ISBN-13 : 978-1-4050-7133-8
FantasticValues ISBN-13 : 978-1-4050-7109-3

Text © Jane Revell, Carol Skinner, 2005
Design and illustration © Macmillan Publishers Limited, 2005

First published 2005

All rights reserved; no part of this publication may be
reproduced, stored in a retrieval system, transmitted in any
form, or by any means, electronic, mechanical, photocopying,
recording, or otherwise, without the prior written permission
of the publishers.

Designed by Pronk&Associates
Page make-up by Pronk&Associates
Illustrated by: Steve Attoe, Robin Boyer, Steve Grey, John Haslam, Kelly Kennedy, Peter Lacalamita, Kim LaFave, Bernadette Lau, Chris Lensch, Roberto Martínez, Dan McGeehan, Bob McMahon, Mike Moran, Mary Peterson, Remy Simard, Sam Ward and Paul Weiner

Cover design by Roberto Martínez

Commissioned photography by Maurice Parkinson/Lucid Photographic p8, 16, 26, 34, 44, 52, 62, 70, 80, 88.

The author and the publishers would like to thank the following for permission to reproduce their photographs:

Alamy/Annet Van der Voort p36b; Ardea/Ian Beames p10c; Bananastock p64; Corbis/Richard Cummins p10e, Corbis/Shai Ginott p46 (camel), Corbis/Charles Jean Marc p36a, Corbis/Mark A. Johnson p18b, Corbis/Wolfgang Kaehler p46 (elephant.ind), Corbis/Catherine Karnow p28a, Corbis/Barry Lewis p72b, Corbis/Peter Turnley p28b; Digital Vision pp 10f, 46 (cheetah), 46 (elephant.af), 46 (panda); John Foxx pp 10b, 10d; Getty News & Sport p54 (rugby); Ingram Publishing cover (dolphins, planet, raccoon, satellite, sky, sledge, windmill); Latin Stock cover (galaxy, wheat field); Nature Picture Library/Sue Daly p90b; Photodisc pp 10a 18a, 46 lion, 46 (giraffe), 46 (chimp), 54 (skate), 46 (ice hockey), 46 (ski), 46 (water ski), 90c; Topfoto/Image Works p72a, Werner Forman Archive p36d.

Printed and bound in Thailand

2009 2008 2007
10 9 8 7 6 5

Fantastic Values 4

MACMILLAN

Macmillan Education
Between Towns Road, Oxford OX4 3PP
A division of Macmillan Publishers Limited
Companies and representatives throughout the world

ISBN-13: 978-1-4050-7109-3

Text © Macmillan Publishers Limited, 2005
Written by Adriana Ortiz Pelayo
Design and illustration © Macmillan Publishers Limited, 2005

First published 2005

All rights reserved; no part of this publication may be reproduced, stored in a retrieval system, transmitted in any form, or by any means, electronic, mechanical, photocopying, recording, or otherwise, without the prior written permission of the publishers.

Designed by Paul Manning
Page make-up by Paul Manning
Illustrated by Adrian Barclay, Baz Rowell and Val Saunders (Beehive Illustration)
Original cover concept by Roberto Martínez
Cover design by Macmillan Publishers Limited
Cover photo by Ingram Publishing

Printed and bound in Thailand

2011 2010 2009 2008 2007
11 10 9 8 7 6 5

Fantastic Values

Contents

1. Respect — Learn why animals are important to us. 4
2. Happiness — Celebrating is fun! 5
3. Well-being — Enjoy outdoor activities. 6
4. Work — Learn about your history. 7
5. Environment — Help to save wild animals. 8
6. Friendship — Respect people around the world. 9
7. Life — Love your family. 10
8. Cooperation — Follow school rules. 11
9. Personal Improvement — Take care of your teeth. 12
10. Compassion — Protect ocean animals. 13

My Values Record 14

Value 1 — Learn why animals are important to us.

Respect

1 Write. Use the words in the box.

> frogs   sheep   bees

1. These insects are very important to us. They produce honey which is used for different things.
   _____

2. These reptiles eat insects. They can hop very high and they have very big eyes.
   _____

3. These animals give us milk, meat, and cheese. People sometimes use their wool to make clothes.
   _____

2 Complete the message.

Remember! _____ need clean seas and rivers to live in!

When you _____ garbage, put it in the trash can.

_____, and _____ are important

for _____, _____

and _____.

Teacher's Corner: In groups, ask students to list different animals and explain why they are important to us.

Value 2

Celebrating is fun!

Happiness

1 Match and write the dates for each celebration.

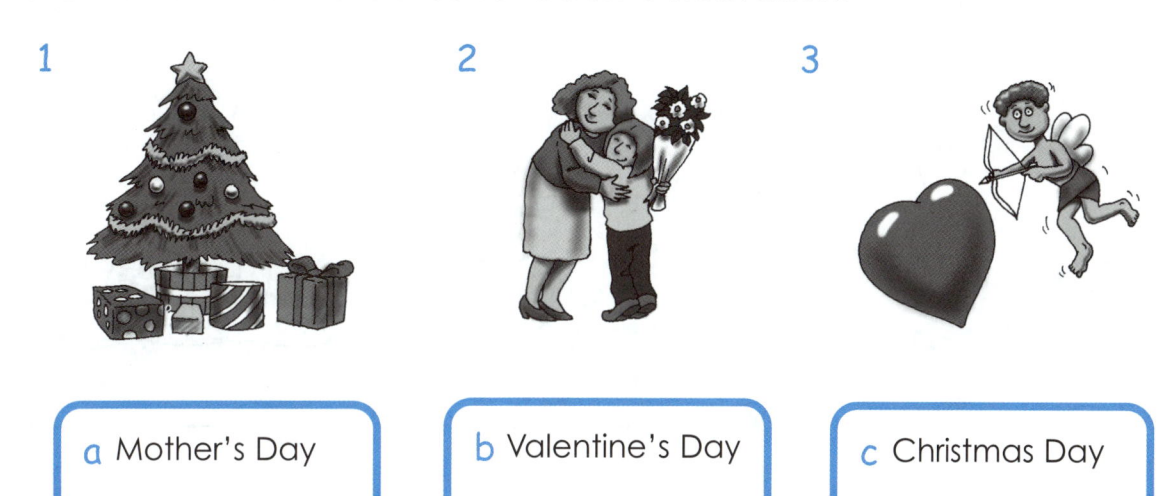

1.
a Mother's Day
_____

2.
b Valentine's Day
_____

3.
c Christmas Day
_____

2 Write three other special days you celebrate.

1 _____
2 _____
3 _____

3 Write about your birthday. Then draw a picture of it.

I love my birthday
because …
_____
_____
_____
_____

Teacher's Corner: Encourage students to work in groups and plan a big celebration for the class. Have them decide who they will invite, where it will be and what they will eat.

Value 3 — Enjoy outdoor activities.

Well-being

1 Label the outdoor activities.

> picnicking   water-skiing   fishing

1 _____   2 _____   3 _____

2 Answer.

What outdoor activities can you do at camp?

At camp I can _____.

3 Complete the following sentences.

My favorite outdoor activity is _____.

I like it because _____.

Teacher's Corner: Have students list fun outdoor activities that can be done in their area.

Value 4

Learn about your history.

Work

1 Complete the sentence. Use the words in the box.

> present   future   past

Know your _____ to enjoy your _____ and make a better _____.

2 Put the pictures in the correct order.

a. ☐   b. ☐   c. ☐

3 Read. Then answer.

> "It's not easy to remember all the facts, but I think history can be fun. I think learning about the past can help us to make a better future."

What do you think about history?

I think _____
_____ .

Teacher's Corner: Ask students to write three historical facts about their country.

Value 5 — Help to save wild animals.

Environment

1 Complete the sentences. Use the words in the box.

> smaller   faster   taller

1 Cheetahs are _____ than any other cats.
2 Giraffes are _____ than ostriches.
3 Chimpanzees are _____ than gorillas.

2 Read. Then circle *True* or *False*.

The African Elephant

The African elephant is the largest land animal. A hundred years ago there were 5,000,000 elephants but today there are only 500,000! People hunt elephants for their ivory tusks. They also destroy the environment where elephants live, so there's no food for elephants to eat.

1 The African elephant is the largest land animal.　　True　　False
2 People hunt elephants for their meat.　　True　　False
3 We need to protect the elephant's environment.　　True　　False

Teacher's Corner: Have students write three ways to help save an endangered animal.

Value 6 — Respect people around the world.

Friendship

1 Label the countries on the map. Use the words in the box.

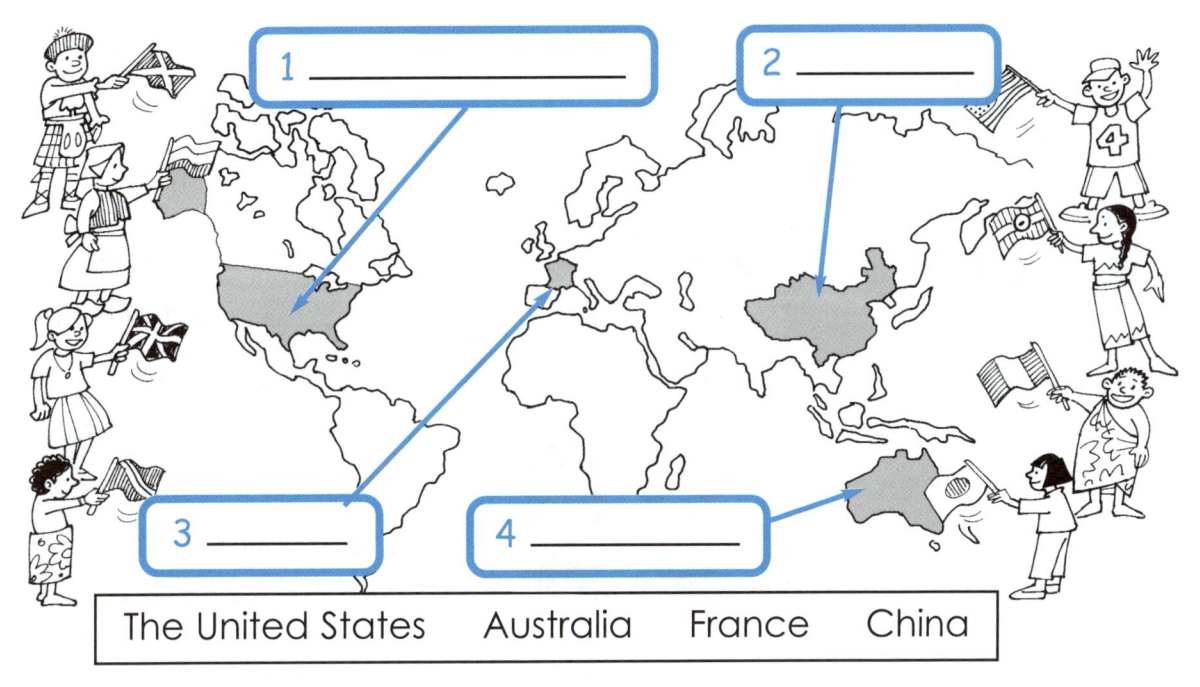

1. _____
2. _____
3. _____
4. _____

| The United States   Australia   France   China |

2 Choose a country you want to learn more about. _____

3 Write a letter to a new friend asking questions about the country you chose in Activity 2.

Dear _____,
My name is _____ and I am _____ years old.
I live in _____. I want to learn more about _____. My country is _____ .
Write me soon,
_____

Teacher's Corner: Have students talk about somebody from a different country. What's the same? e.g. language, food.

9

Value 7 — Love your family.

Life

1 Help Miriam to describe her family tree.

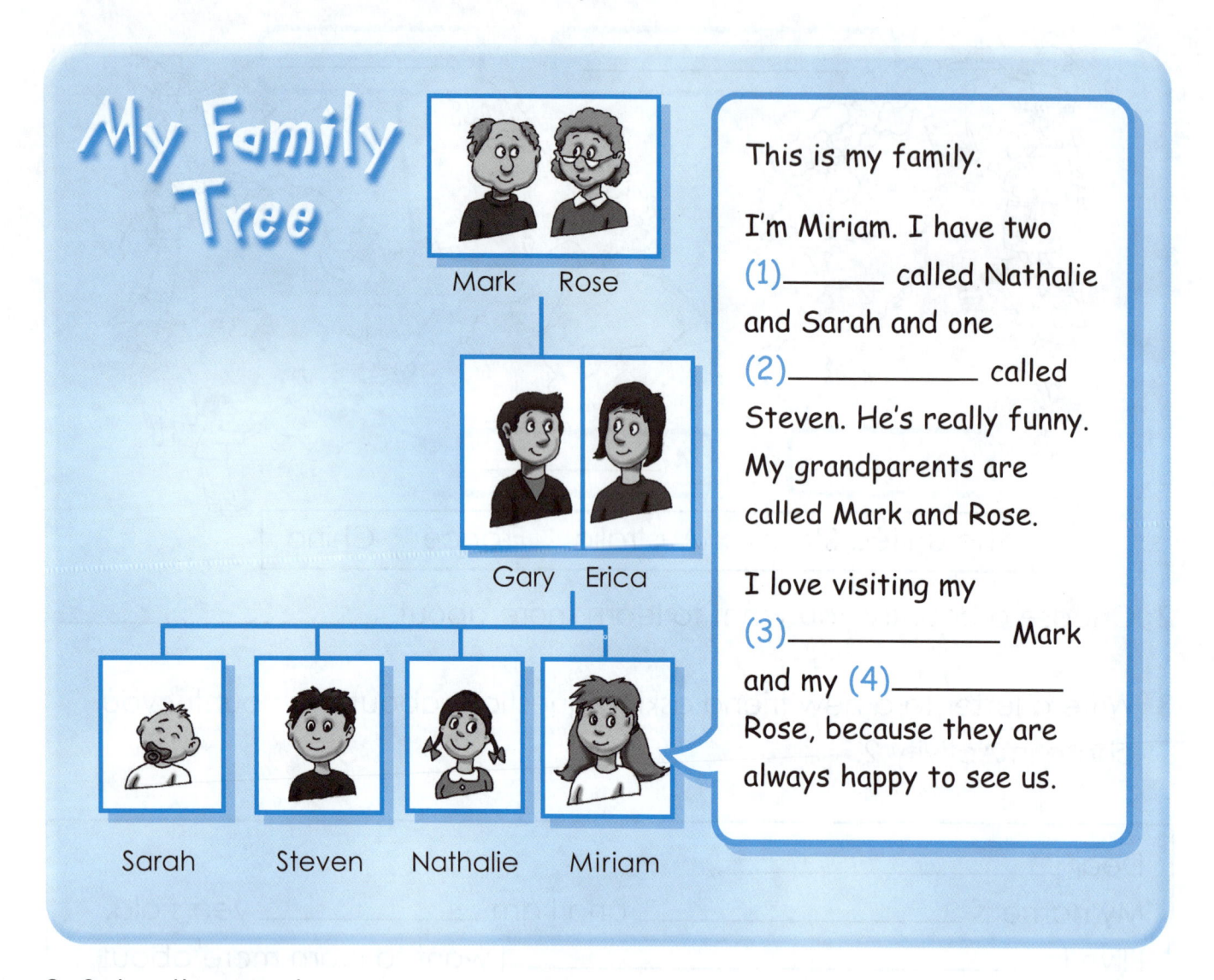

My Family Tree

Mark Rose

Gary Erica

Sarah Steven Nathalie Miriam

This is my family.

I'm Miriam. I have two (1)_____ called Nathalie and Sarah and one (2)_____ called Steven. He's really funny. My grandparents are called Mark and Rose.

I love visiting my (3)_____ Mark and my (4)_____ Rose, because they are always happy to see us.

2 Solve the puzzle.

Carla and Henry are Tommy's parents. Tommy is Liam's dad. Simon is the son of Tommy's brother.

What is the relationship between Simon and Liam?

Simon and Liam are _____.

Teacher's Corner: Have students ask questions about a friend's family and draw his/her family tree.

Value 8

Follow school rules.

Cooperation

1 Complete the rules. Use the words in the box.

> run   push   shout

1 Don't _____.   2 Don't _____.   3 Don't _____.

2 Write a list of three rules at your school.

1 _____
2 _____
3 _____

3 Look at Activity 1 and circle *True* or *False*.

1 It's good to shout loudly in school.   True   False
2 It's not safe to run up and down the stairs.   True   False
3 The boy wanted to wait in line.   True   False
4 School rules help us work better.   True   False

Teacher's Corner: Ask students to decide which school rule they think is most important and complete the sentence "The most important school rule is … because …"

Value 9

Take care of your teeth.

Personal Improvement

1 Complete the words.

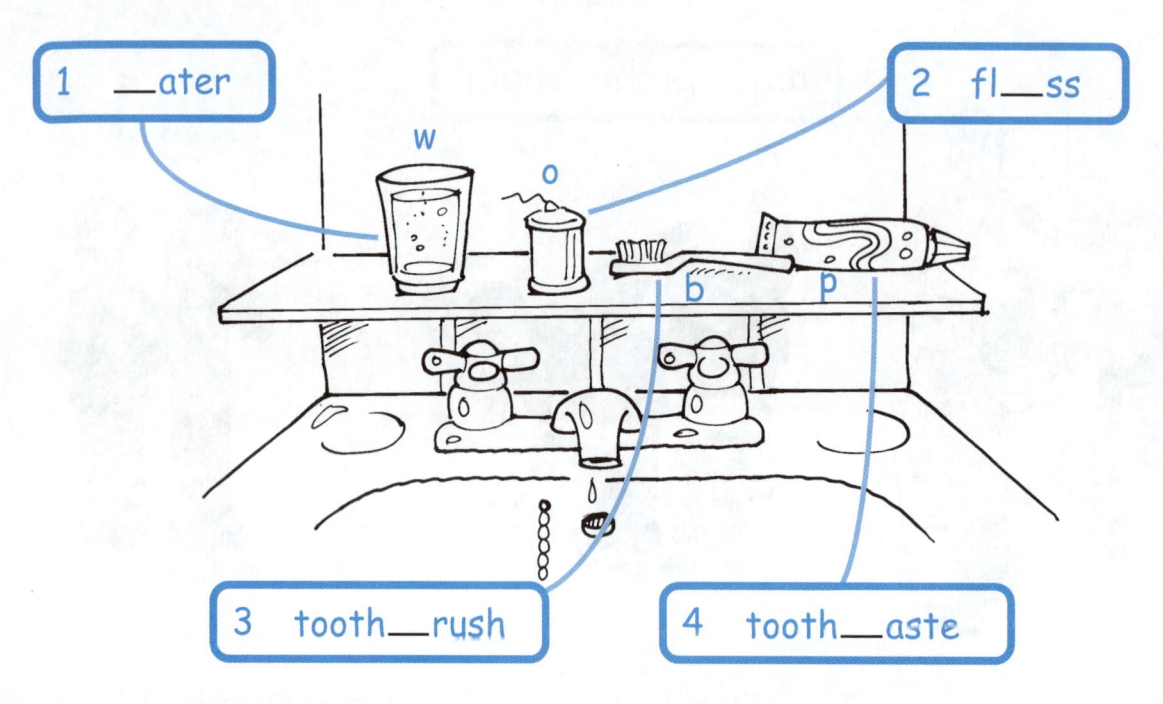

1 __ater
2 fl__ss
3 tooth__rush
4 tooth__aste

2 Look at the pictures and circle which one is correct.

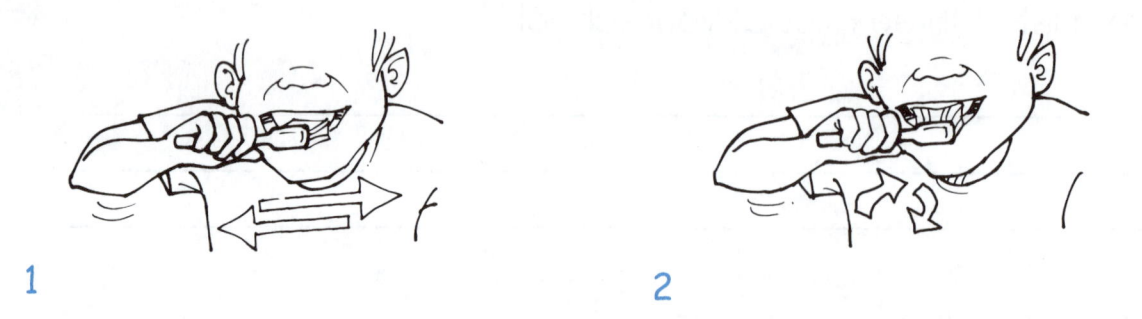

1

2

3 Answer the following questions. Ask a friend if you need help.

1 How many teeth do you have? _____
2 At what age did your first tooth fall out? _____
3 How many times a day do you brush your teeth? _____

Teacher's Corner: Ask students to look at the four things in Activity 1. Then ask them to talk about the best order to use them in.

Value 10 — Protect ocean animals!

Compassion

1 Draw three ocean animals. Then label them.

2 Look. Then put the words in order.

wrong / into the ocean. / to throw / It's / trash

1 _____

need clean water / to survive / Fish and / in the oceans. / other animals

2 _____

Teacher's Corner: Have students write two different ways to help keep the oceans clean.

13

My values Record

Value 1 — Respect

List three things we get from cows.

1 _____
2 _____
3 _____

Value 2 — Happiness

Make a birthday card using only recycled materials.

Value 3 — Well-being

Write two outdoor activities you did last week.

1 _____ 2 _____

Value 4 — Work

Draw or paste a picture of somebody important from your country's history.

Teacher's Corner: After each Value page, have students complete the corresponding My Values Record.

Value 5

Find a picture of your favorite animal and paste it here.

Environment

Value 6

Draw the flag of a country you want to visit.

Friendship

Value 7

Make a list of the birthdays in your family.

_____   _____

_____   _____

_____   _____

_____   _____

_____   _____

Life

Value 8

Make a sign for "No shouting."

Cooperation

Value 9

Draw a poster with the title "Take care of your teeth."

Personal improvement

Value 10

Make a list of five ocean animals.

1 _____ 2 _____
3 _____ 4 _____
5 _____

Compassion